DISASSEMBLY
REQUIRED

A FIELD GUIDE TO
ACTUALLY EXISTING CAPITALISM

GEOFF MANN

AK PRESS 2013

Disassembly Required:
A Field Guide to Actually Existing Capitalism
By Geoff Mann

© 2013 Geoff Mann
This edition © 2013 AK Press (Edinburgh, Oakland, Baltimore)

ISBN: 978-1-84935-126-3
e-ISBN: 978-1-84935-127-0
Library of Congress Control Number: 2012914348

AK Press	AK Press UK
674-A 23rd Street	PO Box 12766
Oakland, CA 94612	Edinburgh EH8 9YE
USA	Scotland
www.akpress.org	www.akuk.com
akpress@akpress.org	ak@akedin.demon.co.uk

The above addresses would be delighted to provide you with
the latest AK Press distribution catalog, which features several
thousand books, pamphlets, zines, audio and video recordings,
and gear, all published or distributed by AK Press. Alternately, visit
our websites to browse the catalog and find out
the latest news from the world of anarchist publishing:
www.akpress.org | www.akuk.com
revolutionbythebook.akpress.org

Printed in the United States on recycled, acid-free paper.

Cover by John Yates | www.stealworks.com
Interior by Kate Khatib | www.manifestor.org/design

CONTENTS

Acknowledgments

The book you hold is the product of many minds (and twice as many hands, I suppose). I would love to take sole credit for it, but ultimately the flaws are the only thing I worked out on my own. The good comes from the sharp eyes of my coworkers, students, and friends. The project began with the Purple Thistle Institute, an alternative to university run in the summer of 2011 by the Purple Thistle Centre, a youth collective in East Vancouver. The participants in the Institute brought energy and insight, and gave me the motivation I needed. I thank them all, especially Dani Aiello, who subsequently joined the Thistle collective and has been a continued help and support (as have the folks who work at the coffee shops where I did a lot of the writing, especially Derek Mensch, whose endless curiosity is a real inspiration). A few people in particular have dedicated a lot of critical energy to some complete version or another of this, and all of them have helped make it a whole lot better, especially Michelle Bonner, Kate Khatib, Carla Bergman, Matt Hern, and Sanjay Narayan.

Carla and Matt, the people behind the Thistle, are the reason this book exists. They have been enthusiastically encouraging me since I began writing, and I don't think I have ever told them how important that has been. In addition to motivating me at the start, Matt also led me to AK, and to Kate Khatib and Charles Weigl, my awesome editors. Everyone at AK has been excellent, but Kate and Charles have gone above and beyond. So much of their work is here that I kind of feel like a co-author. Where I work, I have long leaned on Eugene McCann, Roger Hayter, Nick Blomley, Paul Kingsbury, and Ian Hutchinson (and, just as heavily, on Joyce Chen, Marion Walter, and Liliana Hill). As a "teacher" (I put it in scare quotes because it is not always clear who is teaching whom), I have had extraordinary luck, in the form of Becky Till, Calvin Chan, Emily Macalister, Michelle Vandermoor, Rebeca Salas, Stuart Hall, Victoria Hodson, Mark Kear, and Chloe Brown. Not every teacher is so fortunate, and I am very grateful. In addition, Nik Heynen, Scott Prudham, Jake Kosek, and Brett Christophers are all you could ever wish for in a most enjoyably unprofessional "professional" community. The word "colleague" does them a disservice.

I would also like to extend a special kind of gratitude to Geoff Ingham, whose work has long been a great motivator, and from whom I have learned an extraordinary amount. Geoff has also been a steadfast supporter of my own efforts, despite the fact that most of the time I am merely following in his footsteps. Anyone who knows his writing, especially his excellent book *Capitalism* (cited throughout) will immediately see crucial similarities between it and this book in terms of structure. Geoff has constructed the most elegant structural solution to the complex question of what constitutes the key parts of capitalism, an answer from which I drew the initial inspiration for the first part of the present work. For this and much more, I cannot thank him enough. We may come to different conclusions, but I hope very much that he will find echoes of himself in here, that he will recognize how important all his work has been to me, and that he will be proud of what he has helped bring to life.

Whether at work or beyond it, this book and anything else would be impossible without my family (extended Manns, Bonners, Dyers, and Mobbs), my friends in Vancouver (Panos, Ziff, Matt, Selena, Jess, Ry, John V., Mark J.), teammates (Specials, Generals, and Meralomas), and all the ICSF moms and dads with whom I spend countless hours shooting the breeze on rainy soccer sidelines. Finally, I am especially grateful for the friendship of Andrew Frank, Sanjay Narayan, Joel Wainwright, Brad Bryan, and Jessica Dempsey. They are who you hope everyone finds along the way. They back me up, they laugh their heads off with me, they love my kids, and drink beer at my kitchen table. I can tell, every time I see them—which is nowhere near enough—that they would do anything for me, and I sure hope they know I feel the same about them. Jess, Joel, and Sanj have played a key role in this project in particular, and much of it is the result of many long, late-into-the-night conversations with them.

Which brings me to my Michelle. Everyday I am reminded how amazingly lucky I am to grow old with her, and I just seem to get luckier (and older) by the minute. No small part of her is in this—she is much of the hope and humour I find in what can sometimes seem a dark road ahead. This book is dedicated to the source of the rest of that hope and humour: our two wonderful madmen, Finn and Seamus, the best disassemblers you'll ever meet. It is to them and their friends that the task of reassembly falls. That, at least, is great news, because we are in very good hands.

PART 1

1

An Introduction to Actually Existing Capitalism

In the chapters that follow, you will find what I hope is an engaging and reasonably detailed explanation of contemporary capitalism. It is not an exhaustive or neutral explanation. While it tries to unfold and explain some of the fundamental claims of modern economics, including a few "technical" details, it is not an "objective" description of capitalist economies. In that sense, it is different from titles like "An Introduction to Capitalism" or "Economics for Beginners" currently lining bookstore shelves. Those books can be helpful, in a limited way. At best, they can lay out the "how it works" of capitalism as clearly as any Lego instruction manual. But they almost always substitute an account of how capital says the economy works, or ought to work, for an account of how it actually works. They introduce a whole set of mainstream, "business pages" concepts as if they are unquestionable, the only way to understand capitalism. Those of us driven by a sense that what capitalism offers is nowhere near good enough, and that we can and must create something better, will find little if anything to work with.

This book provides lots of facts and explains important concepts and events, but it also provides ideas, challenges, and critique to chew on. It is not another shrill denunciation of capitalism. Those books often leave one feeling that capitalism is simply a massive class conspiracy, a monolithic force of evil for which only really nasty, cruel people could be responsible. It is as if capitalism happens to us, imposed by external trickery. But that is not true. Most of us actively participate in keeping capitalism going every day, and not always unwillingly. Indeed, some of those it seems to serve so poorly—much of the working class, for example—are among its most energetic defenders.

This book is written with the conviction that much of the way we organize the "economic" aspects of modern life is ethically and politically indefensible, and ecologically suicidal. It is also written with the conviction that merely pointing that out, and then waiting for everyone to agree, is a mostly futile exercise. It simply reproduces slumped-shouldered pessimism or smug radicalism, a chorus of self-proclaimed rebels repeating conspiracy stories and sweeping generalizations with which their listeners already agree: "Banks rule the world!" "Capitalism = greed."

Not that all the conspiracies and sweeping generalizations are baseless—but some are definitely hollow, and those that are true are often only symptoms of other, more powerful dynamics. Take the two placard slogans above. Both seem to state the obvious. Modern governments are beholden to the banks and bond markets, and it does sometimes seem that capitalism is driven by "greed," but in neither case is the problem as straightforward, nor the solution as clear, as the indictment makes it seem. Capitalism is much more complex and compelling than that.

This is a fatal flaw in much radical critique of contemporary capitalism. One of my goals is to expose this flaw, and suggest a way that critique and politics can move past it. It is not enough to point fingers, to expose puppet-masters. Doing so may satisfy a sense of fairness, while indulging in the comfort of a black-and-white politics that identifies "the" enemy. But it almost always degenerates into moralizing. High-horse politics, which rely on the claim that "we" are better or more honest or more caring than "them," the bad guys, crudely oversimplify the difficult choices most people make in real life—assuming they have a choice at all. (Not to mention that such moralizing is what conservatives do best).

Perhaps the CEOs of Shell Oil or Citibank are indeed cruel profiteers and super-rich megalomaniacs. Perhaps they really are bad guys. That is not, and cannot be, the basis of a critique of capitalism. Capitalism is neither made nor defended by profiteers and super-rich megalomaniacs alone, nor did they produce the system that requires the structural position they fill. In reality, capitalism is produced and reproduced by elaborate, historically embedded, and powerful social and material relationships in which most us participate. In fact, many of us struggle to maintain those relationships, sometimes with all our might, because we feel like we have little choice. Are immigrant workers who cross a picket line because they need to cover the rent the "bad guys"? What if they are hoping to one day be a boss or factory-owner? Are they merely duped? Are the poor "really" anticapitalists at heart, but just don't know it yet? Would they choose something other than capitalism if given the chance? On what basis could we make that claim?

"We're good, you're evil" strategies can easily undermine mass solidarity, precisely because of those tricky everyday decisions people have to make. Barring a "clean slate" political solution, such as the revolutionary elimination of the "bad guys" (which history suggests is a risky route), I am convinced that the only basis for solidaristic anticapitalist politics is an analysis that makes sense of "complicity." We need an approach that comprehends the various positions and political dilemmas in which people find themselves, and helps them see that these dilemmas are neither inevitable nor necessary— that they can find what they need in different, better ways, through other ways of living and thinking.

So, while it is partly true, for example, that "banks rule the world" through their control of governments, if we want an end to that control, we need to know more than the fact that it exists. Recognizing the reality we face is a crucial first step, but on its own it gets us almost nowhere. What we really need to know is how banks exercise control: how bond markets work, how the state has come to depend upon them, and what we must undo or fix to alter existing structures of power. If we want to get rid of "greed" (because capitalism is held to be exceptionally greedy), we have an even bigger problem on our hands. Only by ignoring all of human history can we blame greed on capitalism, and it is not obvious that capitalist greed is necessarily worse than, say, the greed of Henry VIII or Hernán Cortez, of slave-owners or elites in the Communist Party of China.

The problem is not that capitalism is a conspiracy of greedy people. The problem is that capitalism, as a way of organizing our collective life, does its best to force us to be greedy—and if that is true, then finger-pointing at nasty CEOs and investment bankers may be morally satisfying, but fails to address the problem. We are aiming for more than a world with nicer hedge-fund managers.

Two premises follow from this. First, we need to understand capitalism in more than just a wishy-washy, general way. If we want to change it, whether by tweaking or reworking the whole economic fabric of society, we need fairly detailed knowledge of the how, why, what, who, and where. Second, while critical theories (like Marxism) have a lot to offer, it is just as important to seriously engage *capitalist* theories of the capitalist economy, the ideas that make up modern orthodox ("neoclassical") economics and political economy. In other words, we have to recognize that as capitalism has developed, it has done so in tandem with ideas of human society with which it makes sense of itself.

Without some understanding of modern economic thinking, we cannot understand capitalism, because we cannot understand the logic and analysis that justifies it, that orders its institutions and gives it the legitimacy that has helped it survive and thrive for so long. Capitalism is organized the way it is because of how capital understands the world—an understanding, we must admit, shared by millions of people all over the world. Capitalism is not maintained by mere violence and deception. If it were, it would be far less robust. It is also sustained by a set of institutions, techniques, and ideas about human affairs and social goals that, for many people in the wealthy world, are unquestionable, as natural as gravity. Critics of capitalism ignore or dismiss these ideas at their peril.

This is not as dry as it sounds. The "dryness" of orthodox economics is part of what gives it its power. It seems so boring and technical, so coldly mathematical. Its subtle technicalities—interest rate dynamics, firm structure, pricing minutiae—sound like the province of arrogant experts and self-important businessmen. But behind this curtain lie key ideas and institutions, and we need to understand them. I wager that, if we put them in their broader political context, you will find a lot of it downright fascinating—troubling, certainly, but fascinating.

The book proceeds by laying out the ideas (Part I), and then putting them to critical work in the real world (Part II). In Part I, the rest of this chapter provides the necessary foundations: what exactly is this capitalism thing? Chapter 2 turns to some influential theories of capitalism, drawing from both critical and non-critical or "liberal" political economy. One theme that will emerge is that capitalism is extraordinarily dynamic and robust—arguably more so than any other way of organizing economic life yet realized. Despite a common misconception that it is rigid and unaccommodating, it has changed a lot over time, and continues to change. In reality, there is a range of actually existing capitalisms. This means that despite their persistent influence, some of the older ideas presented in Chapter 2 seem quite poor descriptions of capitalism today, especially regarding finance and credit, which were not always so central.

With this conceptual frame to help organize our thoughts, the next two chapters in Part I consider the principal features of modern capitalism's core institutions and processes. Chapter 3 starts with the essential capitalist institution that usually gets either downplayed or dismissed: the state. It also examines the form and content of money, maybe the most important way in which the state and the market are bound together in capitalism. Chapter 4 contains an analysis of markets in their varieties, and looks at what their "actual" operation can tell us about modern capitalism and the working people and profit-driven firms that play so crucial a role in its dynamics.

In Part II, we move to a broad-brushstroke examination of the recent history of capitalism, with particular attention to the origins and consolidation of global processes often called "neoliberalism" (Chapter 5), and then to "financialization" and the mechanisms behind the "subprime crisis" of 2007–2008 (Chapter 6). In this case, the devil is definitely in the details—but not exclusively. Chapter 7 is partly a reflection, in light of the political and economic crisis in Europe, on what the previous chapters can tell us about the material and ideological challenges facing alternatives to capitalism. It also considers the necessarily experimental and unclear ways we might demand not merely the end of capitalism, but the emergence of something better. Nothing in these conjectures is definitive or guaranteed. But the critic has a responsibility to say where his or her critique might lead. The wisdom and relevance of these propositions will only be visible in retrospect.

Overall, the goal is to understand how and why capitalism works. Only then can we identify levers of change. "How" and "why" are two different questions. The first is a descriptive problem; the second is analytical, and at least partly historical. Ultimately, it is the analytical part that matters politically, because it requires an argument: *these* are the reasons why capitalism operates the way it does; it is *these* dynamics that inevitably fail to meet the needs of many; and *these* are the reasons there are better, fully realizable ways of organizing our lives. The emphasis throughout is on this analytical side; but we can only get there after getting the descriptive side down as well as possible. We need empirical material to work with, an understanding of the nuts and bolts of capitalist dynamics that is not exhaustive, but nonetheless fairly detailed and subtle.

IF CAPITALISM IS SOMETHING, WHAT KIND OF THING IS IT?

The first thing we need to agree upon is that capitalism is something we can name, with distinctive features that distinguish it in non-trivial ways both from what came before and from other contemporary systems of economic organization. Capitalism is one way of arranging human society, of organizing the social relations of production, exchange, consumption, and distribution. We can call this arrangement, as Karl Marx did, a "mode of production," but could just as easily call it a "mode of organizing economic activity," or even simply an "economic system."

All three terms, one might say, get the point across. However, some precision is useful here. First, in today's capitalist societies, "the economy" and things "economic" are depoliticized and oversimplified. For many, the "economic system" refers to specific dynamics associated with production and exchange in formal (i.e., legally recognized) markets. Rarely does it bring to mind things like women's work in the home, the illicit drug trade, or the education system, even though these are significant components of modern capitalism. To understand modern political economic arrangements, we need language that reminds us explicitly of what they involve, and "the economy" or "economic system" do not do that work right now.

The second reason we need specific terminology is the popular association of modern capitalism with "human nature." It is fair to say that many people believe that the capitalist "economic system" is the logical outcome of "natural" human motivations and proclivities. Capitalism is taken not as *an* economic system, but as *the* economic system. Economic questions are taken to be synonymous with questions about capitalism. Indeed, capitalist political economy has become so dominant in our way of thinking that any economic relationship that is not capitalist is assumed to be somehow "distorted" or "fettered" by the state or some other institution. The assumption is that if an economy is not capitalist, it is either backward or underdeveloped (and thus not capitalist *yet*), or it is being purposely prevented from being capitalist, and would immediately "go capitalist" if left to its own. There is no historical evidence this is even close to true. Markets and states and human communities "go capitalist" when organized to do so.

For these reasons, I think "mode of production" is preferable. It flags the fact that an economic system is always a way of organizing *social* relations. Capitalism, communism, socialism, and any other mode of production you can think of are all ways of organizing the production and reproduction of the system itself. They produce and maintain the ways we live. Thinking of capitalism as a mode of production thus allows us to include in the "economic" conversation the gendered division of labour in the household, which produces particular kinds of workers in capitalism. It allows us to recognize that the way we interact with and shape ecological systems is a key part of how we produce and reproduce our societies. It lets us look at the educational system as, in large part, a training in "economic participation." The mode of production concept flags the fact that capitalism is not defined by factories and financial firms—there are both in non-capitalist societies—but by the societal norms and institutions in which they operate.

The point is that even though we often think of "economic" things as outside or different from social things, they are not. Producing, consuming, exchanging and distributing only happen because people do them— and they do them the way they do for lots of reasons that are not, in themselves, "economic." Producing, consuming, working, and exchanging are social in the "actually existing" sense. The people doing all this are not abstract "agents." They are real living people, vital individuals with likes and dislikes and hopes and fears. They are also members of more or less well-defined social groups and societies based in real times and places. They may be from different groups, societies, or places, of course, but no one is from nowhere. And that means that every person and group involved in economic activity participates (at least in some way) according to the norms, customs, and ideologically embedded practices in which they are immersed.[1]

---

1 It would be a mistake, for example, to think there is something inside most of us that rejects slavery (as a way of organizing production) as categorically wrong, that "human nature" is genetically coded to prioritize freedom for all. We refuse to sanction slavery for a variety of reasons today, but "natural" opposition is not one of them. The historical record might as easily suggest the opposite: that we are "naturally" prone to

More importantly, calling capitalism a "mode of production" highlights the fact that there are other, different ways of organizing the social relations of economic life. Feudalism, which preceded capitalism in much of Europe, was one in which economic activity was organized by coercive lord-vassal relations of tribute and protection (and varied widely in the places and times historians call "feudal"). Another mode of production existed as the authoritarian "state socialism" of the former Soviet Union, a mode that most people erroneously call "communism" (largely because those systems misidentified themselves, of course; few would willingly call themselves "authoritarian state socialists").[2]

slavery-like relations. There is no basis for either position. History and social life, not human DNA, determine the status of slavery and every other mode of social organization. We are against slavery today because it is socially condemned, and we have learned, through much struggle and suffering, not to condone it. Slavery, and opposition to slavery, are social relations.

2 The mode of production "box" in which the Soviet Union or today's China should be put is the subject of considerable debate. Some say that both are in fact forms of "state capitalism." I disagree. This is (perhaps fortunately) not the place to enter into this debate in any detail. Let me just briefly say that given the definition of capitalism laid out above, the political-economic system of the USSR clearly cannot be capitalist. Moreover, the state apparatus in the USSR was not dedicated to surplus value maximization, even in its last stages, but to more "political" goals, the first of which was authoritarian control via the aggrandizement of its productive apparatus. "State socialism" would seem to capture this for me. I think even the idea that after Stalin the USSR was capitalist is a red herring meant to lump its failings in with capitalism's and, for some Marxists, to deflect the critique that its failings were not due to its "capitalism," but in no small part to its incompetent socialism. In many ways, it was socialist, really socialist, and that might

WHAT MAKES CAPITALISM CAPITALIST?

Capitalism emerged in Europe from so-called "precapi-talist" modes of production (principally feudal and mer-cantilist) over a period of centuries. There are longstand-ing debates regarding precisely when, where, and why it emerged, how long it took, and who was involved, but there is a general consensus that by the late eighteenth and early nineteenth centuries, what we now call capi-talism was fairly well consolidated in England, and to a lesser extent in western Europe. Capitalism has since diffused, unevenly and incompletely, across the globe. Often it has done so through coercive means, including war and colonialism. In other places and times, it has spread in a less violent manner, either by simply pro-viding people with what they wanted, or because it was embraced by those who believed it was the key to "de-velopment." Consequently, capitalism does not look the same everywhere you go. Societies with other modes of production have inevitably adapted to capitalism, and adapted capitalism to fit. China, for example, has de-veloped a very complicated relationship with capitalism over time, a relationship that continues to evolve.

Identifying the essential characteristics of capitalism is not a simple task. Many of the features of modern economies that appear to be distinctively capitalist—private exchange markets, for example—are necessary

---

very well have been the problem. Suggestions that the USSR's failings are capitalist mischaracterize history: the Soviet Union was not a different spin on capitalism. It was a totally differ-ent beast, in which the capitalist imperative was not necessar-ily primary. This book shows that the term "capitalist" cannot describe it adequately. The closest thing to state capitalism of which I have any detailed knowledge is Mussolini's Italy, and even that is arguably not very close.

features of capitalism, but are not found solely in capitalist conditions. Others, like "fiat" money (money whose value is not based on an underlying commodity like gold), are products of capitalist development, but were also commonly taken up in noncapitalist systems like Maoist China and the post-Revolutionary Soviet Union. Thus, the range of features that define capitalism as capitalism is up for discussion, but I think Geoffrey Ingham has most effectively conceptualized the essentials as: (1) private enterprise for producing commodities, (2) market exchange, (3) a monetary system based on the production of bank-credit money, and (4) a distinctive role for the state in relation to these features.[3]

(1) Private Enterprise for Producing Commodities

In capitalism, commodities in virtually all forms (although not all, as we will see with the state) are produced by private enterprises that are institutionally, legally, and often socially separated from the household and the state.[4] These private enterprises organize production around employing labour to work on capital to produce profit. Those who operate the enterprise often do not own the physical means or the money used by the enterprise. The way profit is produced, and the nature of the relationship between the worker and the capitalist (and

---

3 Geoffrey Ingham, *Capitalism* (London: Polity, 2008).

4 Sometimes specific sets of commodities are produced by institutions other than private enterprise—the state or community organizations, for example—but rarely, if ever, does this situation preclude private business from supplying those same markets. For instance, the state may produce and sell oil (as it does in Canada via the crown corporation Petro-Canada), but this does not mean it monopolizes oil production and supply. For more on this, see Chapter 3.

the management, who are often not either) is the subject of long and heated debate, as we will see in Chapter 2.

(2) Market Exchange

The exchange of these privately produced commodities is based (more or less) on market competition between buyers and sellers. In a market, buyers generate demand, and sellers generate supply. If there are many buyers relative to supply, demand is high; if there are many sellers relative to demand, supply is high. The resolution of this competition between buyers and sellers, between sellers and other sellers, and between buyers and other buyers—however temporary or instantaneous—produces what we call a price: the agreed upon amount of money for which a commodity is exchanged. In other words, prices are not natural or mechanical products of some abstraction called "the market." Prices may be "objectively" determined, in the roughest sense, by the cost of inputs, labour, etc., but all market prices are social artifacts, the outcome of conflict and negotiation between individual buyers and sellers, and between total demand and total supply—the wage, the price of labour, is the clearest example of the social origins of prices.

Another important feature of capitalist market exchange is that all forms of property, labour, goods, and services, including the enterprise itself and/or its potential revenue, are exchangeable commodities. This means that capitalism, as a mode of production, is characterized by a historically unprecedented breadth of distinct and relatively exclusive markets: money and capital markets, labour markets, intermediate goods markets, consumption goods markets, and financial asset markets.[5]

5 Money and capital markets coordinate the supply and demand

(3) Monetary System Based on Bank-Credit Money

None of the above would work, especially on a large scale, without a means of exchange and payment, or money. The money that circulates in money and capital markets—money used for investment or financial speculation—is produced by banks (loaned) for profit (which takes the form of the interest charged on the loan). Financing production and investment with money created via bank loans is unique to capitalism. While enterprises, wage work, and market exchange of the type we just described all existed in limited form before capitalism, their growth—to the point where they now define how things are done across much of the world—was only possible with the emergence of a state-sanctioned private banking system that could provide the necessary capital.

(4) The State

Finally, the state plays a key role—as both help and hindrance—in capitalism. That role is specific to different nation states at different times, but is also generalizable in important ways. The most obvious is sometimes referred to as the state's "police" or "night-watchman" function: the guarantee of the sanctity of private property rights, the fundamental precondition of all market exchange. But there are other roles that will come up often in what lies ahead, if in complex ways, since the state is always a site of extraordinary contradiction. It

for finance capital; labour markets partly determine wages; "intermediate" goods markets involve the things used in production, as opposed to "final" consumption; consumption goods markets are for the things consumers buy; and financial asset markets are markets in the titles to ownership of any form of property which can potentially produce a return: e.g., stocks or bonds.

simultaneously appears as one of the most powerful obstacles to a world beyond capitalism and one of the most immediately useful tools for building that world.

Before we turn to a more detailed critique of these fundamental aspects of capitalism, however, we need to consider the concepts that enable us to even think about capitalism, and the theories that have explained, defended, and criticized it over time. For much of the power of capitalism, and the challenges facing the effort to displace it, are caught up in how it has become "common sense," how easily the profit imperative has been confused with "human nature."

2

Capitalist Political Economy:
Smith to Marx to Keynes and Beyond

The most powerful theories developed to understand capitalist political economy have always played a significant role in shaping it as well. In general, these theories have three basic and related objectives: understanding economic change, development, or "growth"; understanding the distribution of the wealth that growth generates; and (especially recently) understanding how market prices are determined. Despite this common ground, we find a vast conceptual diversity. These differences are only partly "normative," i.e., attributable to contrasting views of how the world ought to work. The more fundamental force behind them is historical conditioning. Depending on their contexts, thinking humans develop certain ideas and not others; they feel compelled to explain certain elements, others they consider less worthy of attention. Even as they shift meaning over time, ideas carry their pasts with them, pasts with built-in limits and potentials that are hard to see. Once revolutionary ideas can come to seem reactionary. Things considered *a priori* or obviously true in one time and place are often open to debate in another.

Thus, as we turn to the foundational ideas of thinkers like Adam Smith, Karl Marx, or John Maynard
Keynes, we must remind ourselves that theories of capitalism are attempts to make sense of dynamic processes unfolding in the world in specific times and spaces.
This sensitivity is essential to any effort to uncover what
work a theory was meant to do, what work it might or
might not be able to do today, and the difference between them.

ADAM SMITH

Adam Smith is often called the first "classical" political
economist. Why "classical"? Marx coined the term to distinguish this mode of "liberal" political economy from
what came before (the "pre-classical"). Earlier economics
(if we can call it that) primarily concerned the size of,
and influences upon, the king's coffers. Classical political
economy, in contrast, developed an analysis of national
wealth as collective or aggregate income, and was interested in the forces affecting the economic activity of the
nation as a whole, not merely that of the monarch.

Smith was both extending and breaking with the
analysis of the Physiocrats, political economists of eighteenth-century France who believed that the natural
productivity of the land, set in motion by agriculture,
was the origin of all wealth.[6] For them, surplus value—
the "additional" value produced between input and
output in a production process—was possible only as
a gift from nature. Their policy conclusion was logical:

---

6 Some of the better-known Physiocrats include Francois
  Quesnay, Richard Cantillon, and Jean-Baptiste Say (of "Say's
  Law," on which more to come in the section on J. M. Keynes
  below).

if agriculture was the source of the surplus upon which the state and all society depended, then anything that hindered it (taxes, trade restrictions, etc.) was bad.

Agriculture was also crucial to Smith, but the physiocratic approach seemed unable to make sense of his context (eighteenth-century Britain). In contrast to the relative conservatism of pre-revolutionary, absolutist France, Smith witnessed a period of extraordinary dynamism in Britain, which experienced a massive shift in the composition of society and an extraordinary accumulation of wealth. Smith's objective was to intervene in a debate about the nature and causes of that change, which was marked by the dwindling success of feudal and especially mercantile systems of wealth accumulation and social organization.

Among the internal changes Smith witnessed, the most important were associated with a remarkable expansion in "commerce," or the pursuit of individual gain via production and exchange by a growing proportion of society. Among the external changes he noted was the collapse of powerful empires and states that had formerly successfully accumulated wealth via the exercise of military power. Mercantilist states organized international economic activity around the "carrying trade," bringing goods from places of production to places of consumption—via the spice trade between Southeast Asia and Europe, for example. Wealth in mercantilism was generated by state-favoured firms enjoying returns from arbitrage—the profits produced by the difference in purchase and sale price (which was of course augmented by colonial exercise). Trade routes and monopoly powers were sanctioned by the state, and protected by military power, tariffs, and other measures.

When Smith wrote his political economy (*The Wealth of Nations* appeared in 1776), the mercantilist system was increasingly crisis-ridden, the most astonishing example being that of Spain—a global mercantilist imperial power—losing control of the Netherlands, the relatively tiny emerging centre of what we might now call "capitalist" finance. Smith wanted to both explain how this new system was working, and determine how the state might help it work even better, to its own and everyone else's advantage.

Like all classical economists, Smith was particularly interested in two phenomena: growth (what caused it) and distribution of income (what determined it). Because he was writing before the explosion of factory production—"industrial" capitalism—he was largely concerned with the expansion in the range and depth of market exchange, and the enormous wealth it seemed to create. His answer to the growth question was that eighteenth-century Britain's wealth was due to extraordinarily productive shifts in the interaction between the "factors of production": land, labour, and capital. These also gave him his answer to the distribution question: landlords, workers, and capitalists receive their respective share of the wealth generated by these interactions, in the form of rent, wages, and profit.[7]

These actors, Smith said, were connected in a "circular flow": capitalists and workers paid rent, capitalists paid wages, landlords and workers consumed, and capitalists made profit, starting the process over again.

---

7 "Factors of production" is still a common term in economics today (although one hears much less about land). The term "economic growth" has, however, only been in common usage since World War II.

The factors of production—and thus the classes that depended upon them for income—were mutually dependent. They had to exchange with each other, or nobody would win.

Smith thus argued that "freedom" of exchange and price determination (which would allow this system to work smoothly) were essential to the new system's success. If we all depend upon maximum interaction, then anything that hinders it is by definition bad. And since it appeared that a new "liberty" among the population had made these exchanges possible (relative to feudal and slave modes), it seemed likely that the lack of state coordination (which for Smith would have been synonymous with "monarchical control") made it possible. Although (by my reading, at least) he only uses the phrase once, this is what Smith meant by his famous "invisible hand": the hand that made real wealth possible was neither the king's nor anyone else's. The implication, to some, was that it was God's.[8]

According to Smith, circular flow engenders increasing market specialization. Producers seek to meet identified needs, creating an increasing division of labour, which allows for greater efficiency in the production process, which lowers costs and meets the needs of an expanding market. This is also supposed to work at the international scale. David Ricardo's later elaboration of Smith's theory led to the idea of "comparative advantage," i.e., nations will specialize in the production of what they are best at (in terms of cost or efficiency).

Smith assumes that in this system, money serves almost entirely as a means of payment or unit of account.

8 Adam Smith, *The Wealth of Nations* (New York: Modern Library, 2000), 484–85.

He doesn't imagine market participants seeing money as a form of wealth they could or should accumulate (as we would today). This leads him to assume that people will not hold money as a store of wealth, but will spend it, keeping the circular flow going. Although Smith didn't say it outright, in this system, price—the temporary resolution of competition between market participants—serves as a *signal*: rising prices tell producers to produce, and falling prices tell them to stop producing, or to produce differently. In addition, when prices are rising, new producers will enter a market and purchasers will leave, and when prices are falling, producers will leave and buyers will enter. Thus, price signals ought to lead automatically to "equilibrium" and the full employment of resources: any leftover resources would clearly be cheap, and would therefore find a price at which they made sense, eventually allowing the system to put all its productive capacity to work.

With all this working so well on its own, Smith does not see a big role for the state—basically, it needs to protect the nation, enforce the law (especially property law), and provide some public goods (i.e., infrastructure like roads and bridges). Still, it is a complete mischaracterization to suggest he saw no need for the state, as one often hears from people who claim to be working in his tradition. The state remains essential. This kind of thinking played a crucial role in the justification of Britain's international role in the nineteenth century, which we might call "free-trade imperialism." Smith himself took his logic to suggest that colonial power was not always what it was cracked up to be, and he supported the American desire for independence, suggesting the North American colonies be given representation in

British Parliament, join a "federal union" with Britain, or better, be entirely emancipated from colonial rule.

KARL MARX

Smith and his followers are why we use the term "neoclassical" to describe modern economists who argue that the market is the most efficient and fair way to distribute.[9] They are, or at least see themselves as, the "new" Smithians (but with a couple of important twists, as we will see). But not all Smith's admirers have been market fundamentalists. Marx, for instance, is sometimes thought of as the anti-Smith, but if we look at their ideas, they are not so radically opposed. The most important difference between them lies not in their explanation of what drives capitalist production, but in the fact that Smith saw increasing harmony and mutual interdependence where Marx saw conflict, exploitation, and inequality. In his analysis of capitalism—and remember, unlike Smith, he wrote after the rise of the terrible factory system— Marx emphasized the tensions and conflicts endemic to capitalism, both in the relations between capitalists, and between capitalists and workers.

Marx called these processes "contradictions": opposing or conflicting forces, whose interplay would eventually produce new forms, which would themselves contain their own contradictions. He argued that it was the force of these contradictions, the inability of any system to stay put in some steady state, that drove historical change in and through different modes of production. For example, as the technical and organizational forces

---

9 The term "neoclassical" with respect to economics was coined in 1900 by the American economist Thorstein Veblen, the same person who first discussed "conspicuous consumption."

of production change over time, they become less and less compatible with social relations that developed on the basis of earlier ways of doing things. The contradictions that emerged mean that eventually the relations must be reconfigured, sometimes radically.

Marx explained basic capitalist dynamics in the following manner. First, he adopted from Smith a distinction between use value and exchange value. Things that humans use labour to produce virtually all have a value "in use," something you might do with it, like a hat you wear or a loaf of bread you eat. In any exchange system, things produced by labour also usually have a value "in exchange": you can get something from someone else by trading them. In a monetary system, capitalist or not, producers sell things with use value on the market (if they didn't have use value, no one would buy them) and receive money in return.

The two values do not have to be equal; indeed, they never are, since they represent two completely different phenomena. Use value is qualitative and non-generalizable; how do you measure the "usefulness" of a hat on your head, and if you did, would it be the same measure for everyone? Exchange value is clearly quantitative. In fact, that is basically all it is, a quantitative indication of an object's value in exchange. What you can get for it can be very diverse, like in barter. Or it can be socially standardized, as in, say, 1 hat = 10 buttons. In either case, only exchange value is quantifiable, and, according to Marx, money emerges in a society when one commodity becomes the standard quantitative measure of exchange value. He calls that special commodity the "general equivalent," because it is seen as quantitatively equivalent to any other commodity. It is the commodity that everyone understands as the one thing that can be accumulated, or piled up, in amounts that, in value terms, are socially accepted as equivalent to anything tradable. There is no reason money has to take any particular form; we could use buttons for money if everyone accepted them as money.[10] Of course, how we come to accept money as money—do we "decide" democratically, or are we "told" authoritatively?—is an important question, to which will we turn in Chapter 3.

Marx considered the distinction between use value and exchange value essential, because in capitalism, in contrast to many other modes of production, wealth is accumulated in the form of exchange value: i.e., money. In other times and places—for example, among pre-conquest First Nations of the North American Pacific Northwest, where I live—wealth was accumulated in the form of use-values. To be wealthy meant possessing assets considered valuable, like food and clothing and slaves. (In some of these First Nations, the powerful demonstrated that wealth by giving it away "for free" in a ceremony called "potlatch.") By Marx's time, only money or assets readily convertible into money counted as wealth in Europe and North America.

One defining feature Marx noted about the world in which he lived was the glaring difference between people's opportunities to accumulate wealth, and hence

---

10 This helps explain some interesting features of monetary history that sometimes confuse us moderns, like the enormous stone "coins" of some ancient cultures. These were not money as we understand it today; rather, in essentially non-monetary social formations, "monetary" exchange was confined to very specific exchange conditions. These involved, unsurprisingly, significant ceremony—like the movement or change in ownership of a ten-ton "coin."

to enjoy security and a full and happy life. These differences depended on what people had to do to put food on the table. While virtually everyone has some capacity to contribute labour to producing things with use and exchange values, few both have the capacity to labour *and* own the stuff labour needs use to produce things—land, natural resources, tools, factories, etc. I might have all the skill and energy in the world, but without lumber, a hammer, nails and some wire, I cannot build a fence. You might be the most talented chef in the land, but without stoves, ovens, pots, utensils, and food, your hands are idle. These things that help us produce other things (and the money to purchase such "means of production") have a special status. They are the magic things that, mixed with labour, turn raw materials into other materials for use and exchange. This special relation is what makes them *capital*, and makes the smaller group of people who own and control them *capitalists*.

What needed explaining, according to Marx, was why there were capitalists at all. Why didn't everyone have, or at least have access to, those things that enabled you to produce things for use or exchange? How did the capitalists get to be the ones with the tools and resources? In search of an answer, he looked at European and especially English history. In light of those histories, he argued that capitalists and capitalism arose through a series of processes he called "original accumulation" (a phrase often translated less helpfully as "primitive accumulation"). By forcefully asserting a property right over what had been collective resources—enclosing common land, appropriating raw materials from colonized peoples, etc.—the means of production became concentrated in the hands of a few. This left the expropriated many with no means of getting by on their own. To survive, they had no choice but to find a way to get access to the means of production, which are also the means of putting food on the table.

One the most important conclusions Marx drew from this historical analysis is that capital can only exist in relation to its opposite, labour. Original appropriation by the few from the rest not only meant the emergence of capital, but also of wage labour. Once dispossessed, the many can get access to the means of production only by offering their capacity to work to the capitalists, in return for payment in some form. Selling one's energy and skills for wages on the "labour market" is the source of one of the most important features of capitalism according to Marx: the distinction between labour and labour-power. Labour is the specific or "real" act of working. Labour-power is the abstract "capacity to work": skills, knowledge, energy, etc. specific to each of those without access to means of production except through capitalists. Wage workers do not sell "living labour," they sell the commodity labour-power on the labour market. The capitalist, who thus comes to control one more thing necessary for production (and the most important one at that—human energy and ingenuity) puts that labour-power to work as he or she sees fit, and pays the workers a wage for each unit of time they give up the control of their human energies.

Capitalists use labour-power, in combination with the means of production, to produce commodities for market exchange. (Commodities are, by definition, things produced for sale on the market—if you grow carrots to put in your salad, they are not commodities.) By selling commodities for more than it costs to produce them, capitalist profit is made possible. This is why Marx emphasizes capitalism's social relations, and not merely its technical features, like, say, "advanced industrial machinery." It is not technology or the form of firms' "capitalist" organization, but property and other relations that define capitalism as capitalism. Capital is a social relation insofar as it is the nature of something (money, land, equipment) which, combined with human energy, has the capacity to expand or increase the amount of exchange value in the context of a particular arrangement of property relations and production systems.

This argument is the source of Marx's well known exchange formulae: C-M-C and M-C-M'. Basically, his point is that in "pre-capitalist" modes of production, commodities were exchanged in order to get other commodities; the goal was not to accumulate money except insofar as it allowed you to purchase other commodities or accumulate wealth in another form, like gold or jewels or land. This C-M-C (Commodity-Money-Commodity) exchange made sense if one was a monarch and wanted to hoard precious metals and property, but it also characterized "everyday" transactions.[11] If, for example, you were a saddle-maker, and you wanted to eat, you sold saddles for money, and used the money to purchase the commodities you ate, among other things.

With capitalism, Marx says, the fundamental unit of exchange relations changed not just quantitatively, but qualitatively. Capitalist production and exchange is not a high-powered version of its "pre-capitalist" antecedents, as modern orthodox economists tell it, but a different thing altogether. Capitalists start not with a commodity they have produced and seek to trade, but

---

11 W-G-W, *Ware-Geld-Ware*, in Marx's German.

with money, with which they purchase commodities (including the key commodity, labour-power) to mix together in a production process that produces other commodities, that are then sold for *more* money: M-C-M' (M' being original-M-plus-something-extra).

Marx thought one of his key insights, if not *the* key insight, was that this process of profit-making—capitalists selling commodities for more than it costs to produce them—shows that the "extra" or surplus value created in the production process comes not from capital's contribution, but from the labour power workers contribute to the whole relationship. In other words, the appropriation of labour's surplus value—you can pay them less than what they produce is worth—is the source of wealth in capitalism.

This idea—the basis of the so-called "labour theory of value" (a phrase Marx never used)—is a very big deal. Yet it is frequently misconceived, both by those who think they agree with it entirely, and those who think it mistaken. Interestingly, these contrasting views do not sit on one side or the other of a simple left-right divide. Many on the left reject the labour theory of value, and many on the right accept it, if unwittingly. But either way, in most cases it is misunderstood. Contrary to what it might seem to suggest, Marx is definitively *not* arguing that labour produces all wealth in all times and places. His point is almost the opposite. If Marx has a "labour theory of value," it pertains to capitalism alone. Only in capitalism is labour the sole source of *value*.

The misunderstanding is partly due to the fact that "value" in everyday English is generally considered to be a "good" thing. In addition to something that has some monetary worth, we frequently describe something "substantive" or "positive" as having "value." Consequently, when we hear that Marx thought labour produced all value, many of us think Marx thought all good and useful things come from labour, and the problem with capitalism is that despite this essential contribution, capital rewards labour unfairly. This resonates with many a lefty's "progressive" intuition. But Marx said neither of these things. What he actually said is much more insightful and important.

For Marx, "value" is the form wealth takes in capitalism. Value is precisely that abstract, monetized, everything-has-a-price-if-you-dig-deep-enough quality that many decry. It is the generalized relation of equivalence among all those qualitatively different dimensions of the world, rendered in cold quantitative form and expressed in money. Value is the tacit but astoundingly powerful relation that enables us to make an AK-47, an SUV and a field of grain exchangeable as "equivalents": e.g., 100 AK-47s = 10 SUVs = 1 field of wheat. If you think about it, this is remarkable, and somewhat terrifying. My example is in no way absurd; indeed, the political economy underlying much of the current land-grab in Africa consists in exactly this exchange of equivalents: arms, elite luxury goods, and agricultural land. Capitalism's historical achievement is to create a systematic and seemingly natural set of social relations that uses labour not to produce useful or beautiful things for the good they provide—if it did, then the "value" of those three things could never be rendered equivalent. Instead, capitalism condemns labour to produce "value" in this specifically capitalist sense.

If we work together to plant a community garden that can feed its members and add something useful to our lives and relationships, we would very comfortably say our efforts produce something valuable. Marx would never deny that, but it has nothing to do with what he meant by value in capitalism. Indeed, he would have said it is a good thing precisely because it does *not* produce capitalist value, but instead produces what he sometimes called "real wealth," things that truly contribute to human physical and social well-being. The sources of real wealth are not only human, of course: nature, Marx noted, has a big role to play.

Similarly, it is certainly true that capitalism treats workers unfairly, and any improvement workers can realize in their lives is a "good thing." But capitalism is not a bad system just because the numbers are off. For Marx, capitalism is bad because it is a systematic set of social relations in which humanity is prevented from realizing its capacity for "real wealth," human potential, justice, and a non-arbitrary distribution of the means of life. (In fact, capital's defence of arbitrary distribution, a kind of Darwinism that says that those who are wealthy are "by nature" the fittest in the economic ecosystem, is one of its main self-justifications.) If higher wages were all that is necessary, Marx would have been no more than a wordy and over-philosophical union activist. The problems, however, are much bigger: the wage relation and capitalist social relations themselves. The point is not to redistribute capitalist value, but to overcome it, to destroy it as the relation that rules the world.

The idea that capitalism will persist as long as the rule of value holds is Marx's essential lesson. This is not a majority opinion, and is easily taken as dismissive of "reformist" efforts to improve working conditions and the distribution of income. I don't mean to suggest such efforts are useless because they are not "radical" enough. Clearly, any effort on the part of labourers (and unemployed people) to improve the material conditions of their everyday lives is worthwhile. My point is that the fundamental problem with capitalism as a mode of production is not ultimately addressed by the redistribution of *capital*.

I suppose it is possible to argue that, while the rule of value is not fundamentally challenged by individual struggles to increase labour's share of wealth, we might yet use such a strategy to sentence capitalism to "death by a thousand cuts," as it were. Perhaps redistributing capitalist value more fairly, i.e., paying workers what they "really" deserve, might somehow undo capitalism as a mode of production. Maybe it has some built-in constraint that renders it structurally unable to pay "fair" wages to all workers, and if forced to, it would effectively collapse under its own weight.

It is not exactly clear what Marx thought about this strategy. He supported struggles for higher wages and better working conditions, but he also thought that no matter how high the wage rate, the wage relation itself is an essential pillar of capitalism, one that must be knocked down to create a post-capitalist world. If nothing else, he would probably have pointed out that there are some tricky contradictions involved in thinking that rewarding people with higher wages will lead them to toss off the very system now paying them "fairly." The whole point of paying workers well is to keep the system going—in fact, there is a theory in orthodox economics that says this is exactly what "fair" wages do. So as a social justice strategy, wage demands are key. As a social transformation strategy, they are insufficient.

Yet it must be said that this still does not suggest an obvious reason to reject the idea that if workers were paid "fairly"—presumably at least as much as capital-ists—then no one would want to be a capitalist any-more, or would have no self-interested incentive to be one, and the whole mode of production would fall apart. In other words, we might use the wage relation to overcome the wage relation.[12] This resonates with Marx's belief that capitalism's undoing would come about from inside: the post-capitalist world he felt inevitable—even if he could not tell when it would come—would emerge not through an attack on capital from outside of capi-talism, but from the collapse of the social relations that maintained its internal coherence. Ultimately, the main Marxian lesson is that we cannot reach a post-capitalist world unless we forsake, either willingly or because we must, the very relations that define capitalism as capital-ism: value, capital, and wage-labour.

AFTER MARX: THE NEOCLASSICALS

Marx is sometimes included among classical political economists because he uses the same categories (value, capital, and wage-labour) found in the political economy that came before him. Putting Marx in the classical box might be convenient, but it is more mistaken than help-ful. Marx's whole point was to critique political econo-my as a way of knowing, not to redo political economy in a "critical" way. He may have used the concepts the classicals developed, but he historicized and destabilized them in ways they could never have imagined.

---

12 One thing to keep in mind, however, is that it would have to be all workers who enjoyed this transformative wage; history suggests that if it is just a fraction of workers, then the lucky few who earn "enough" tend to become much less interested in transformation.

Be that as it may, the distinctions between Marx and his predecessors do not much clarify the definitively non-Marxian "neoclassical" political economy that came after him. Most of it was largely unaffected by his thought, at least directly, and was thus not only different from Marx, but developed in ignorance of his analytical contribution. Instead, it represented a very different, liberal reaction to the same classical political economy against which he reacted so strongly. The most important differences between this liberal or neoclassical political economy and the older work of those like Smith and Ricardo lie in those "twists" on Smith's classical take that I mentioned above.

The first twist is in the theory of distribution. There is a stark contrast between classical theories of political economy that understand prices and exchange as a function of the social relations of production and the neoclassical perspective that they are determined by demand. In fact, the well-known neoclassical doctrine that "without interference" markets will function perfectly (or "clear") is also known as "demand theory." The second twist is in the theory of value: while the classicals took capitalist value, the relation of general equivalence, to be inherent in some material substance or human action, the neoclassicals understand it as "subjective," determined by individual tastes. It is worth considering each of these "neo" twists in some detail, because it is almost impossible to exaggerate how crucial they are to modern economics' analytical justification for capitalism.

Neoclassical Twist #1: Distribution

For the classicals (in this, at least, we can include Marx), political economic analysis must be founded in society's relations of production, exchange, and consumption. Of course, thinkers like Smith, Ricardo and Thomas Malthus (perhaps the most famous classical political economists) did not understand their analyses as specific to their historical and geographical context, but assumed their logical universality. They took nineteenth-century England as the historical and geographical centre of the world, and thus they thought they were not writing about just any old place, but about a "modern" set of economic relations that was clearly the direction in which history was headed. This is what Marx meant when he said that classical political economy was formulated as if everyone was, or at least acted like, a petit-bourgeois Brit: in one translator's rendition, an "English shopkeeper."

Universalized or not, social relations are the classical basics. Despite the wide range of policy goals classical political economists advocated, all their analysis was oriented toward developing a theory of distribution between the various classes involved in production (labour, capital, and landlords). The point was to explain who gets what and how much, in contrast to "neoclassical" economics. Figuring out what determined prices was a secondary concern.

Perhaps the most important steps in the transition from classical to neoclassical political economy lie in what is sometimes called the "Jevonian revolution." Although named after William Stanley Jevons, the term in fact describes a shift in economic reason to which many contributed. The Jevonian revolution definitively ended the hold of "who gets what," class-based analysis in orthodox economics, and instead consecrated the individual "consumer" as the unit of analysis. Like most mainstream economists to this day, he treated individuals and their preferences as ultimate data, neither produced by nor dependent upon anything but each person's subjective and autonomous decisions regarding what they needed and what made them happy. This change is crucial, especially because it shifted how "who gets what" was understood. In the classical analysis, the distributional question is answered by what each *class* contributes to production. Labourers get wages, capitalists get profit, and landlords get rent. Even Marx, who felt that capital managed to get its share by "using" the commodity labour-power, understood distribution as determined by socially dominant definitions of each factor's relative contribution—the amounts received are relative to the (capitalist) value of their "input."[13]

In contrast, Jevons said the answer to the distribution question is *not* determined in production, but in exchange, by prices that reflect individually "given" preferences. Different individuals (forget about classes) get what they can pay for. And what they can pay for is determined by the price of what they want, which is in turn a function of how much there is, and how badly they and others want it. The market, not social relations (like property), determines distribution, and in an entirely objective, "natural" manner. This is a radical

---

13 It is interesting to note that Marx argued that the "valuation" of labour's contribution to capitalist production processes could not be called "unjust," since the meaning of justice is determined by the social relations of production in specific historical conditions. In capitalist society, "justice" is a capitalist standard. There are no "unjust" wages in capitalism, according to Marx; what was unjust (and clearly not by capitalist standards, but by the revolutionary ethics Marx espoused) was the wage relation itself.

change. On this account, the market "decides" without a "decider"; it makes no promises, and it cares nothing for "justice" or what a particular contribution "deserves." This means distribution is a secondary concern, worked out after price formation, which is a function of supply and demand (and obviously therefore the ability to pay).

It impossible to underplay how important this change turned out to be for life in modern, capitalist societies. The neoclassical doctrine is basically a bald claim that distribution is somehow *not* a function of, or really even affected by, social power and property relations. Instead, we are told, who gets what is determined outside those processes, in the neutral, apolitical, and un-manipulatable field of the market. This is a critical step toward the idea that "the market" is "natural" and "disinterested"—the principal, maybe the only, basis upon which the word "market" can be paired with the word "free."

Neoclassical Twist #2: Value

The shift from classical to neoclassical political economy dramatically reconfigured the dominant understanding of value, in a manner very different from Marx's distinctive critique. Classical economists like Smith and Ricardo held to the labour theory of value we discussed above, the one many people associate with Marx (who granted it a great deal of ideological force, but saw that as why it was necessary to abolish it). Their theory was that things have value in proportion to the amount of labour that goes into producing them. If something takes a lot of time, effort, and skill to produce, or if no one wants to do it, it will cost a lot; if it can be cooked up in a jiffy by anyone, it will be cheap.

They did not posit some naïve labour-time price calculation, of course, but argued that labour value describes something like an average, and it will vary by time and place. They also understood that if something is relatively easy to produce, but producing it requires tools that are labour-intensive to produce, then the "total" labour involved will be reflected in a higher value.

Beginning with Samuel Bailey in the mid-nineteenth century, and Jevons a little later, political economists rejected this "substantive" theory of value (i.e., labour is the "stuff" of value). Just as Jevons transformed the theory of distribution in an individualized "consumer" manner, they argued instead that value is not determined "objectively" by stuff-amounts, but "subjectively," by individuals' tastes and preferences. If people want a lot of it, and want it badly, it has a lot of value, and its price—the expression of value—will be relatively high, and higher still if there is little of it to go around. This idea—that abstract, uncoordinated, decentralized forces of supply and demand determine the value or price of a commodity—is the foundation of modern mainstream economic analysis. When modern orthodox economists talk about the theory of value, they mean the theory of price determination.[14]

---

14 For those familiar with a little bit of economic terminology, this is the basis of what is now called "general equilibrium" theory, the hallmark of modern neoclassical analysis. The "general" part refers to the entire set (the "vector") of prices within an economy. The idea that those relative prices can find a system-wide equilibrium is the heart of the neoclassical theory of value, a theory often called "Walrasian," after the seminal contributions of Léon Walras, a nineteenth-century Swiss economist. Walras did more than perhaps anyone else to reshape economics along the lines of a natural science like physics.

All this depends upon an understanding of the individual, with his or her given tastes and talents, as the atomic unit of human life. This idea is the foundation of the common sense that informs contemporary economic understanding, the basis upon which modern economic institutions and policy are considered legitimate and logical. It is no exaggeration, I think, to say that although you don't hear people walking around talking about value and distribution, these theories are the logic behind the form capitalist institutions take. The idea that the distribution of socially valuable assets, resources, and so forth is a product of individuals pursuing their subjective self-interest, in combination with Smith's "invisible hand," leads easily to the normative proposition that unrestricted individual pursuit of self-interest produces, almost despite itself, optimal collective well-being.

These ideas helped justify a social philosophy called utilitarianism, which originated in the mid-eighteenth century, and whose last bastion is modern economics, where it continues to exercise a mind-numbing stranglehold in the form of "welfare economics." Utilitarianism explains all human action as a motivated by the quest for pleasure and the flight from pain. Consequently, it proposes perhaps the simplest theory of human welfare imaginable for both individual and the community. It works like this: people act rationally when they maximize their self-interest or "utility" (given certain constraints, like how much money they have). Since those interests are subjectively determined, whatever you are

---

If we had to choose one text as the foundation of modern, mathematized, neoclassical economics, it would have to be his *Elements of Pure Economics* (1877). "Pure" presumably meant "assuming away all that complicated real-life stuff."

doing, it is probably a utility-maximizing choice. The corollary, of course, is that the community is merely a set of individuals making these calculating choices, and community "welfare" is measurable only by the maxim "the more utility, the better." Because utility is experienced entirely at an individual level, no distributional or fairness problem arises. If you add pleasure, even if only for individuals who already have a lot of it, it's all good. You are not "taking away" from someone else. In fact, many utilitarians claim that added utility, even if it increases inequality, will eventually "trickle down" to those who didn't get the extra to begin with.

In combination, these conceptual tools—rational pursuit of self-interest, clearing markets in which prices are determined by individual tastes, the invisible hand—form the core of modern "economic" knowledge, and its assertion that markets can make predictability, calculability, stability, and equilibrium possible.

JOHN MAYNARD KEYNES

From the early 1800s to World War II virtually all orthodox economists and "statesmen" in Europe and North America camped somewhere in the neo/classical range. The Great Depression that began in 1929, however, initiated a massive shift in what ideas were considered acceptable. So began the Keynesian era, named for the "revolutionary" work of the British economist John Maynard Keynes (1883–1946). We shouldn't exaggerate the abruptness of the change. There were forerunners to Keynes' ideas, and his took some time to become common sense. Classical/neoclassical ideas and policies persisted into and after the Depression. But there is no denying that between 1929 and the end of World War

II, the world of political economy was transformed.

The key theoretical break turned on the theory of money. Orthodoxy had come to be associated with *laissez-faire* liberalism, a commandment to the state to "let them do as they will": "free markets," "free trade," and unfettered pursuit of self-interest. Laissez-faire thinking understands money basically as Smith did: as a convenience for exchange and a way to make accounting easy. Money exists so that instead of me bringing my piano to market, and finding some combination of barter exchanges that ends with the fishing-net I want, sale and purchase can be separated in time and space. Accordingly, the orthodox economics of Keynes' time assumed money had no utility as wealth, only as a convenience. It was economically neutral, a "veil" over the "real" economy. It made no sense to hold on to it; one would naturally put it back into circulation as soon as possible to enable the Smithian circular flow of wealth generation.[15]

When the Depression hit, Keynes (who had long defended this older thinking), saw that these ideas were just plain wrong: people wanted to hold money more than other stuff. They were buying less, investing less, and in general keeping the money and money-like things they had (things easy to use in exchange, like gold). And that, he said, should never ever happen if classical economics is right. Money was clearly *not* neutral, but had a very real, and fluctuating, value of its own as a security in the face of uncertainty. If money had ever been neu-

---

15 As we will see, the end of Keynesianism, and "return" of neoclassical economics in the postwar era, has also involved the reassertion of the theory of monetary neutrality, although it is now dressed up in a range of complex conceptual costumes (e.g., money-in-the-utility-function) that obscure it.

tral in the classical sense (something he doubted), it was no longer. Modern capitalism, he said, is a "monetary production economy," and money was perhaps its central institution, much more complex than a convenient means of payment and accounting device.

Like most of his ideas, Keynes arrived at this conclusion via what he thought was simple common sense. Yes, he said, it is true that from a purely utility- or profit-maximizing perspective it makes more sense to use one's cash holdings to consume and invest. But because the future is always uncertain, it makes sense, in the real world, to hold at least some money most of the time, and a lot of money at especially unstable times. Keynes called this propensity to hold assets in money form "liquidity preference," "liquidity" being the ease with which an asset can be readily monetized, i.e., exchanged for money. So if "liquidity preference" is high, it suggests people feel insecure or uncertain, and do not want to be holding on to assets they will have trouble selling if things go south.

Keynes argued that the state of liquidity preference among market participants, fluctuating in response to everything from weather to war, exercises enormous influence on modern monetary economies. The stock market, for example, enables rapid purchase and sale of highly liquid assets—indeed, the whole point of the stock market is to turn an enterprise, which on its own and as a whole is about as "illiquid" as it gets, into a collection of easily exchanged units of property. This is, of course, extremely useful and appealing to stock-holders, but difficult for the firms in question, whose bits and pieces are picked up and dropped in a flash—often for no apparent reason other than investors' whims (a volatility only exacerbated in the "information age"). This is only one example of how prone capitalism is to what we might euphemistically call "inefficiencies." It is one of a whole suite of dynamics that make the fundamental assumption of classical and neoclassical economic theory—that markets clear, resources are fully employed, and all engines are running full-bore—a highly improbable description of the world. Full employment, if it ever happens, will not hold for long. Keynes was pretty sure that, at least since the beginnings of capitalism, it had *never* happened.

The idea that "free markets" will realize capitalism's "full potential" is proven wrong by more than just investors' uncertainty. Fundamental features of capitalist institutions are also responsible. Keynes showed this, for example, in his demolition of the orthodox theory of unemployment. If we assume (as many orthodox economists do) the market economy would run at full capacity were it not for "inefficient" individual or state decisions, then any unemployment is due to the free choice of unemployed individuals. Remember utilitarianism? Here is a good example of the role it plays in orthodox economic analysis: unemployment represents a "preference" for leisure (that is really the word used) over available jobs at existing wages.[16] But if Keynes was right, and money is kept out of circulation due to uncertainty, then much if not most unemployment is

---

16 It sounds crazy, but this idea still circulates in powerful circles. Not only do some modern economists still believe it—see the passages below on the Chicago School—but even those who don't must assume that if it weren't for "imperfections," markets would be perfect, and there would be no idle resources, like unemployed workers, hanging around.

involuntary. This hurts both workers and employers, by reducing consumer demand and investor profit expectations, which means they will not buy and invest enough to get the economy running busily enough to pull all the workers into jobs. The changing intensity of unavoidable uncertainty regarding the future makes it impossible to expect that somehow everyone will just "get over it" and get the economy going full steam ahead.

The older, Smith-Ricardo-Jevons traditions knew levels of activity could decrease, but they said that if prices, especially wages, decreased too, then firms would start producing, investing, and hiring again, workers would be pulled into jobs, and everything would be hunky-dory. But, Keynes said, look around at the capitalist world in which we actually live. Prices don't adjust that easily: workers either resist wage cuts, or, more likely, even if they are willing to accept them, as many in the Depression were, they cannot coordinate any economy-wide reduction in labour costs anyway (it's not like they have that power in capitalism). Investors won't instantly become optimists and throw their capital into production and hiring. For any set of self-interested actors, there is a massive collective action problem. Often, he said, the only answer is for the state to step in as mediator, regulator, and coordinator of economic relationships: organizing labour and capital so as to manage consumer demand, planning investments so they are complementary, and providing stimulus in the form of government spending when consumers and investors start to feel insecure again, as they inevitably will.

According to Keynes, this suboptimal up-and-down, occasionally with really high ups and really low downs, is how capitalism works. Its volatility is not a result of mismanagement or interference or workers' demand for "excessive" wages, but a part of how it functions "naturally." And, if the capitalist state does not manage the ups and downs, people might become so disgruntled that all that communism and socialism stuff whispered about in field and factory starts making sense. In the middle of the Depression and then World War II, with the Russian revolution in the background, that warning made many capitalists sit up and take notice. They may not have been big fans of liberal democracy, but it beat the alternative.

More on this later (Chapter 5). But before we turn to the principle institutions of capitalism, it is worth noting that Keynesian ideas, in different forms (not all of which Keynes would have endorsed), dominated capitalist economic theorizing from World War II until the early 1970s. Explicitly Keynesian theory and policy fell with the rise of a reinvigorated, formally complex ("mathematical"), and strident form of neoclassical analysis that was the first step toward the capitalist ways of knowing and doing we live with today. The crisis that began in 2007 has certainly troubled this resurrected neoclassicism, but, despite their obvious flaws, there is no guarantee that neoclassical economics or the neoliberalism it underwrites will go the way of the dodo.

3

State Power and the
Power of Money

This chapter and the next analyze four key components of capitalism—the state and money (Chapter 3), and markets and firms (Chapter 4)—to show their interdependence and contradictions. All are essential to capitalism's remarkably dynamic history, and to its robustness in the face of so much change. While it is clearly important that these relations interlock effectively enough to produce a real "system," at the same time, the ways they fall short of the dreams of orthodox economics are, in some cases, the reason the system works. Sometimes, the elements of the capitalist mode of production that fail to fully play their assigned role actually help the system reproduce itself. In fact, if capitalism worked exactly as some orthodox theories suggest, it would not have lasted very long at all.

THE STATE

Capitalism is premised upon two kinds of power: (1) private economic power that comes from the control of property and profit-making; and (2) coercive power exercised by states in (and often beyond) bounded national territories.[17] These two types of power exist side by side, but they have an inconsistent relationship, by turns complementary, conflictual, or indifferent. There are, however, a couple of things we should keep in mind about them.

First, we should be clear what power means, and how the two kinds work in practice. I am using the word "power" in the somewhat mainstream sense to describe authority or control and the way in which it is exercised, not in the "positive" or "productive" sense associated with influential French philosopher Michel Foucault. In other words, I mean both the form power takes, and the ways it is held.[18] So, when we think of private economic

---

17 I borrow these categories from Geoffrey Ingham's excellent book, *Capitalism*.

18 On Foucault's account, power, as a relationship between various groups and individuals, produces forms of social life, including the individual subject. I choose a more "common sense" notion, however, partly because I think that the way Foucault's ideas have been taken up, this "mainstream" sense gets forgotten, even though it remains enormously important in everyday life. I also think Foucault's ideas have been somewhat misconstrued in English because he was talking about much broader relational phenomena in his work. It is true that Foucault approved its translation as "power," but the French term *pouvoir* means more than "power"; it has the additional sense of "capacity." His early account of power is clearly not aimed to specify the realm of state power with any precision. When he turns to the question of state power in lectures near the end of his life, the sense I give it here fits with his account very well. Indeed, his explanation of liberalism as driven by the principle of "the maximum limitation of the forms and domains of government action" only makes sense with this more mainstream concept of state power in mind. Michel Foucault, *Birth of Biopolitics: Lectures at the Collège de France, 1978–1979* (New York: Picador, 2008), 21.

power in capitalism, we are thinking of the form that power takes and the ways it is exercised, i.e., the power enterprises and individuals can exercise over human relations by means of their access to, possession of, and/or control over money, means of production, labour power, etc. They exercise this power in an attempt to help things turn out the way they prefer.

When we think of state power over territory, we think precisely of what defines the state as the state. In sociologist Max Weber's classic definition, the state is that set of institutions which enjoys "the monopoly of the legitimate use of physical force within a given territory."[19] This power is coercive: the state, by virtue of its control over the police, law, military, etc., has the power to coerce you, if you are inside its territory, to do or not do certain things, and to punish you if you don't follow the rules, which the state itself determines. Virtually all capitalist states limit these powers via laws, constitutions and "bills of rights," for example requiring the police to have a warrant to enter and search your home. But the state (at least in theory) remains the sole possessor of this territorially defined coercive power.

One of the key features of modern political life that anticapitalists must think hard about, however, is the fact that in capitalist liberal democracy, state power is rarely straightforwardly coercive. In practice, states require, and actively seek, legitimacy from their citizens. Through a variety of mechanisms—the most obvious are elections—capitalist liberal democratic states try to build some consensus around their power, so that subjects see it as fair, right, or natural. Indeed, I would

---

19 Max Weber, "Politics as Vocation," in *From Max Weber: Essays in Sociology* (Oxford: Oxford University Press, 1946), 78.

suggest that any attempt to create a mass-based oppo-
sitional politics, at least in the global North, will fail if
it frames liberal democracy as simply an instrument of
elite class rule or as a fancily-clad capitalist police state.
There are moments—like the oppressive response to the
G-8 protests in Genoa in 2001—when it might seem
so, but in terms of a larger and more incisive political
critique, the state = coercion argument is shallow, and
has limited purchase.

This is not to say that the coercive part goes away.
You might think, quite reasonably, that since coercion is
always hovering in the background, the consent part is a
bit of a joke: if you don't consent, you get coerced, meaning the consent is not all that consensual. At the level
of the isolated individual, this is true. But if you think
about it at a collective level, the consent part is much
more evident. If every single person refused to consent,
the state's coercive power would almost certainly be insufficient. The stability of the liberal democratic state
as an institutional complex depends on the often tacit,
sometimes explicit endorsement of its citizenry. Modern state power is constituted by a complicated, shifting,
and contingent combination of coercion on the part of
the state and consent on the part of the population.

On a related note, it is not only the state that can
coerce. Private economic power rarely lacks some coercive aspect. Think of the power your employer has
over you, or the power that the banking industry has
in contemporary capitalism. Market power (the power to influence price determination and revenue flows;
discussed in detail in Chapter 4) and the employment
relation both have coercive elements that work through
the supposedly consensual exchange relation. Banks can

push through laws in their interest because they can use their market power to disrupt the whole economy—to coerce the government to meet their demands. Your boss can require you work faster, or smile wider, with the threat of losing your job. That is coercion.

The combination of coercion and consent (operated by both capital and the state) produces a relation known as "hegemony," a term first elaborated in this sense by a justly famous pre–World War II Italian communist named Antonio Gramsci. Gramsci spent the last decade of his life in Mussolini's fascist prisons, during which time he penned a remarkable collection of notebooks that have, since their posthumous publication, joined the ranks of the most influential works of radical political thought ever written. Gramsci was the kind of radical anticapitalist theorist that even those opposed to "theory" admire, since his theoretical efforts were always aimed at making sense, for political work, of the concrete contexts in which struggle unfolded. I cannot recommend reading his prison notebooks highly enough (and for those familiar with his work, you will hopefully recognize his inspiration in this book).

Gramsci worked out his idea of hegemony while he was reading the work of Lenin, trying to understand the means through which communism might reconfigure the political and ideological terrain of interwar Europe, Italy in particular. In that context, fascism *and* liberal democracy seemed to direct the to and fro of everyday life so powerfully that, in many instances, the state and its allies did not even need to monitor the security of capitalist social relations. Those relations seemed so natural to most people that they reproduced the system themselves. In Gramsci's formulation, this was a product of capital's hegemony, its power to shape the "common sense" we tacitly share about the state, the ruling classes, and their power: that those relations are natural, that they serve a necessary function, that they are the only way to keep the peace. Those in power construct an effective hegemony when the existing order appears to be not only in their interests, but in everyone's interest. It is the practices that render a given social formation ideologically "normal."

The main point is that when thinking about the two constitutive logics of power in capitalism, we must remind ourselves that neither of them are "pure." Many ways of exercising power coexist, and none can be separated from other axes of social difference that have been used to dominate different times and places, such as racialization, patriarchy, and nationalism. Nevertheless, I believe it is helpful, at least as a "first cut," to think of the two types of power as having different dynamics. They also have specific spatial implications.

The spatial dimension often gets overlooked, but it is important. Different types of power operate in, and produce, different kinds of space.[20] On the one hand, power in capitalism can focus on bounding and exercising control within specific territories. Inside that bounded space, whether it be the home country or a colony or something else, the state does its thing, controlling, deciding, coercing, convincing, etc. When those exerting this kind of power want more of it, they tend to try to expand the territory, so that it includes more people and resources. When the state exercises its authority in this way, capital can clearly benefit by producing goods

---

20 Here I am drawing heavily on the work of Giovanni Arrighi, especially *The Long Twentieth Century* (London: Verso, 1994).

and services in the territory, extracting natural resources and distributing them between the colony and the metropolis, and so on. This "territorial" logic, in which the state and capital cooperate, benefits both. The Spanish colonial era of the fifteenth and sixteenth centuries is a clear example of this logic: Spain territorially enclosed much of the Caribbean and the Americas in the interests of accumulation in the home country and in elite colonial outposts. This kind of power persists in our post-colonial time, for example, via the global expansion of consumer markets and production and supply chains overseen by multinational corporations like Nestlé, or by "conditional" development grants like those doled out in Africa by the Canadian International Development Agency (which require the local state to contract Canadian firms for the development work). The increasing dominance of nominally "foreign" markets and resources by capital and states based in the global North is as spatial as it is an "economic" process.

The second logic of power and space, which arguably characterizes today's financial capitalism, is less about controlling territory, than controlling flows between or across territories. This logic of power can also be enjoyed by the state and capital together, since the state benefits greatly from the wealth generated by capital when it compels and directs the flows of goods and services. Think of the wealth generated in London and New York by the fact that those cities are the hubs of the modern financial system. England and the US would not be as globally influential as they are without this power, which is not territorial in the colonial sense. Of course, recent US and UK imperial forays in the Middle East again demonstrate that there are no pure types.

We should also note that these power dynamics are not necessarily well-coordinated or complementary, either on the part of capital-as-a-whole or capitalist nation-states. Different states and their domestic capitals can pursue different logics at the same time. For example, Spanish colonial power died at least partly because the Dutch took control of the ways that Spain financed its ventures—flows of capital beat territorial colonialism. Alternatively, US imperialism in the Arab states has long irked UK capitalists, who, though untroubled by the imperialist core of the US program of action, feel as though they were "there first" (and indeed, it was British imperialism that created many of the states in the Middle East).

In light of the history of these logics of capitalist power, Ingham makes the crucial point that it was precisely the territorial competition between states (in sixteenth- and seventeenth-century Europe, when the modern state system started taking shape) that led to the adoption of national debt as a way to finance military ventures for territorial conquest. Since the debt was financed by the emerging and newly powerful bourgeoisie—the first real capitalists, who increasingly had the money the state needed—this arrangement gave both the state and (what we would now call) capital an interest in each other's long-term welfare. The state needed a healthy bourgeoisie to lend it money, and the bourgeoisie needed a healthy state to generate profits on its investment in government debt, in access to new resources and markets, and in production (which requires the social peace the state's coercive power helps ensure).

This development is the basis for Ingham's most important argument: that this interdependence of the state and its capitalist class is the historical source of the "common sense" understanding of the two as relatively autonomous spheres of social life. Since both the state and capital depended on the welfare of the other, they agreed to leave each other to their respective spheres. If capitalists demanded "freedom"—i.e., laissez-faire economic arrangements—and had the money the state needed to finance its war and imperial conquest, then it made sense for the state to back off. And in return, if the state provided capital with protection of its property rights and essential infrastructure for commerce (like roads), then it made sense to let the state do its thing.

In this relationship, the state (the realm of formal institutional "Politics," with a capital "P") came to be understood as providing the social container for the realm of activities we now call "the economy." By the mid-seventeenth century, at least among the European bourgeoisie, "Politics" and "the economy" were no longer understood as one set of phenomena associated with the functioning of the national collective, but as two distinct realms of collective life. It is a basic argument, for instance, of Thomas Hobbes' *Leviathan*, an occasionally notorious, oft-misunderstood, and enormously influential tract published in England in 1651. Although what Hobbes was "really" trying to say is still debated, there is general consensus that one of his key claims is that a self-sufficient "civil society" (i.e., the private economy) can thrive of its own accord only where a powerful state guarantees the social order.

Whatever its historical basis, the idea that the Politics-economy separation is "natural" must be rejected. Indeed, as the briefest critical glance at everyday life suggests, it is a myth (albeit a very powerful one), and any common sense it has today is a historical product of liberal capitalism. There is absolutely nothing inevitable about it. Even granting the fantastical notion that the state is the sole realm of politics (I suppose it is the sole realm of "Politics"), the claim that the state and the economy do not constitute and determine each other was blatantly disproven by the world in Hobbes' time, just as it is disproven today.

But we talk about "the economy" in contemporary capitalism as if it were an independent realm, unaffected, or at least potentially unaffected, by the state and social life more generally, a total and complete impossibility. Yet, precisely because this is how the system is widely perceived, it is crucial to consider explicitly the work these ideas do. Ingham is very good on this. He says there are three main ways the state interacts with "the economy," and, although they are not so easily separable, the distinctions are useful. They are:

1. State provision/production of social peace;
2. State maintenance of capitalist social relations (often via "liberal democracy"); and
3. Direct and indirect state participation in the economy.

Social peace is both a precondition and a goal of modern capitalist hegemony, and the state is a crucial—but not the only—means by which social peace is maintained. This is not to say, however, that capitalism can only develop in a "peaceful" context. Nor is it to say that the coercive power in capitalism sticks happily to its own "proper" realms of social relations, like policing or the justice system, leaving markets and their participants to "peacefully" pursue their interests. There are times, for example, when capitalist markets—which are supposed to be purely "consensual"—can operate in a context of more coercion and less consensus, and forms of coercive power can certainly move into "spheres" of social life where in theory they do not belong—markets in Mafia protection are a good example. Yet, while capitalism can sometimes work in such contexts, they are not indicative of the capitalist state's relation to "the economy." Mafia hits in Moscow and Russian oligarchs' strong-arm expropriation of public wealth via terror and theft is not really hegemony in any meaningful Gramscian sense, and it tells us little about the role of the state.

Successful hegemonic projects necessitate both coercive capacity on the part of the governors and consent on the part of the governed. In other words, the state and the social relations it protects must be granted, at least by a significant part of the population, sufficient legitimacy. *Capitalism requires legitimacy.* What is not so clear, however, is the means through which it acquires legitimacy: are we fooled into acquiescing to capitalism by cultural institutions like the church, or by transactions that cheat us in ways we don't understand? Are we "bought off" by the welfare state, basic amenities, and the possibility of upward mobility? Is capitalism the "best possible" or "least bad" system, thus meriting our reasoned endorsement? Furthermore, to what extent does the state participate in the legitimation process? If we are dupes, is it the state that dupes us? Capitalists? Both? If we are bought off, surely the state is important, but in whose interest is it acting? Is it extracting from capitalists in the interests of workers? Or is it appeasing workers in the interests of capitalists? There is, of course, no one universal answer to these questions.

It seems certain that much of modern capitalism's legitimacy derives from its supposed mutually interdependent relationship with liberal democracy. Liberal democracy is focused on individual rights, freedom of exchange, and procedural consistency (i.e., the rules of the game apply to all members of the polity, including those who exercise state power). It is commonly assumed that liberal democratic states are the optimal means through which to determine, and enforce, the rules of the capitalist game. The provision and protection of property rights is again a great example—without it, capitalist exchange would be impossible. Who would buy something if they could not be sure that after the transaction they will own it? Who would buy something if they could not be sure the seller had the right to sell it? Because liberal democracy did not exist prior to capitalism, many have claimed that the two co-evolved and are necessarily interdependent. According to capitalist reason, it is obvious that you can't have democracy without capitalism, and you can't have capitalism without democracy.

This common sense is not entirely disconnected from the real world, but it is based on selective memory and a naïve overconfidence in our ability to know the future. Consider the following: even if it were true that capitalism and democracy have always gone together (and it is definitively not true), this would in no way justify the claim that they will go together until the end of time. Transhistorical claims originating in particular historical modes of production have never proven true, and there is no reason to expect end-of-history claims about the mutualism of capitalism and democracy are any more correct than previous prophecies.

More importantly, there is an overwhelmingly obvious rebuke to the claim that democracy and capitalism are mutually necessary: the contemporary Chinese political economy. Many analyzes of the Chinese experience, from all sides of the political spectrum, describe present-day China as "authoritarian capitalism."[21] If China is capitalist—and not only is it arguably capitalist, but as Slavoj Žižek loves to point out, it appears to be better at capitalism than anyone else—then the inevitability of the democracy-capitalism marriage clearly does not hold.[22]

The credibility of capitalism's inherent democratic decency is further eroded by the fascisms that spread across Europe and other parts of the world in the mid-twentieth century. This is certainly no small matter: no account of Italy, Germany and Spain in that period can describe them as noncapitalist. Indeed, Germany's remarkable performance during the 1930s, when much of the world was down and out, made fascism very appealing to many at the time, including a heck of a lot of capitalists—and, it must be said, quite a few workers too.[23] Moreover, one cannot attribute the failures of fascism to its incommensurability with capitalism, as if it were a contradictory system never meant to be. Fascist Germany was a capitalist economic growth

---

21 See, for example, Yasheng Huang's *Capitalism with Chinese Characteristics: Entrepreneurship and the State* (Cambridge: Cambridge University Press, 2008).

22 See Slavoj Žižek, "No Shangri-La," *London Review of Books*, volume 30, no. 8 (24 April 2008).

23 There were active fascist parties in many European countries at the time, and they were not all considered right-wing nuts. This was also true in North America, although to lesser extent: John F. Kennedy's father Joseph, for example, was a fascist and Nazi sympathizer, as was the poet Ezra Pound.

machine—cheerfully endorsed by both German capital and much of German labour—that was crushed, thankfully, by the war. However hateful the regime was, there is no evidence that fascist capitalism itself was doomed to failure on its own. Indeed, some have made the compelling argument that fascism helped save German, Italian, and Spanish capitalism in the 1920s and 1930s, by overcoming capital's resistance to full employment, thus providing a "political" solution to a nominally "economic" collapse.[24] When fascism fell, at least in Germany and Italy, it was not due to some flaw in its "variety" of capitalism; it was fascist leaders' hubris, Allied bombing, and internal resistance that killed it. Indeed, *Generalisimo* Francisco Franco, whose victory over the Spanish Republicans in 1939 was partially funded by Texaco and other capitalist firms, peacefully "retired" from almost four decades of autocratic brutal-tyranny-in-capitalism in 1973, bequeathing Spain a degenerate constitutional monarchy and decades of political turmoil.

Add to this the unfolding history of developing-world dictatorships propped up by the US and western Europe over the years—none of which are easily classified as noncapitalist—and any claim that capitalism needs democracy is on shaky ground. It may be that liberal democracy needs capitalism, but it is definitely not the other way around. In fact, whatever anticapitalism's prospects, the future of anything like democracy will depend very much on which of the terms dominates the capitalism-democracy pairing. Even if in the short

---

24 Michał Kalecki, "Political Aspects of Full Employment," in *The Last Phase in the Transformation of Capitalism* (New York: Monthly Review, 1972), 79–80; Nicos Poulantzas, *Fascism and Dictatorship* (London: New Left Books, 1974).

term it seems democracy is tied to capitalism, there is clearly no *necessary* mutual dependence between the two. What is certain is that we can no longer leave democracy to the capitalists (see Chapter 8).

But that does not mean it is merely accidental that the two are so often paired. For Ingham, the origins of democracy lie in the political contradictions generated by the capitalist mode of production. The ideological fundamentals of liberal democracy—"universal" human rights, individual liberties, procedural consistency—were the same as those put forward by the proto-capitalist bourgeoisie in their effort to gain some freedom from the yoke of the state. When these classically "liberal" ideas became culturally dominant, they unsurprisingly trickled down from the elites to the workers and other noncapitalists, who mobilized those ideological tools in their own interests.

This is partly the story of how liberalism became hegemonic, and its plausibility depends on workers having at least some power to realize their interests. This means, despite many "radical" critiques, that the state is not simply a crude instrument of capitalist rule.[25] For the power of liberalism to work as this account suggests, capital cannot entirely dominate and coordinate the state. The exercise of capitalist hegemony via the state must have some degree of popular legitimacy; the state must also hear the workers and the rest of the popula-

---

25 This idea is sometimes attributed to Marx and Engels, who, at the beginning of the *Manifesto of the Communist Party*, argued that the "executive of the modern state is but a committee for managing the affairs of the whole bourgeoisie." This, however, is not the same as saying it is a crude instrument of capitalist control.

tion. This would appear to be a reasonable characterization of the history of many states in Europe and the Americas where democracy appeared.

This idea—that the state in capitalism is not just capital in "public" office—is captured well by Nicos Poulantzas. Inspired by Gramsci, Poulantzas also emphasized the historical separation of the political and economic realms of capitalist social life. He argued that the state, insofar as it occupies the central position in the political realm, thereby enjoys "relative autonomy" from things economic and various classes' straightforwardly economic interests. It is not a mere tool of any particular class or interest, but is linked in different ways to them all, while enjoying some independence at the same time. It is the "factor of cohesion": its relative autonomy from any one class or class fraction is what makes hegemony in capitalism possible.[26] In other words, the state is the complex of institutions through which the contradictions and conflicts that plague life in capitalism are managed. Hegemony, the combination of coercion and consent that allows the interests of one social group to come to stand as the universal interest, is a political practice involving various alliances and relations.

This does not mean the state is neutral regarding capitalist social relations. As we well know, it is far from neutral. Virtually every state institution in the developed world is consciously pro-capitalist (even if it does not speak the word officially). In fact, at one point Pou-

---

26 Nicos Poulantzas, *Political Power and Social Classes* (London: New Left Books, 1973); Nicos Poulantzas, "Preliminaries to the Study of Hegemony in the State," in J. Martin (ed.) *The Poulantzas Reader: Marxism, Law, and the State* (London: Verso: 2008 [1965]), 74–119.

lantzas argues that because the modern state is a necessary means of capitalist hegemony, it is capitalist *by definition*—it is not that the state "manages" capitalism, but that the state *is* capitalist. This is debatable, especially if we want to be more historically flexible in our use of the word "state." But whether we accept this claim or not—Poulantzas himself eventually largely disowned it—the significance of Poulantzas' insights is undiminished. The state's relative autonomy provides a basis for two crucial dynamics in modern capitalism. First, it enables the state to solve problems that squabbling and back-stabbing among competitive, self-interested capitals could not or would not solve—think money provision, state enterprises, and public goods. Along these same lines, it invests in so-called "human capital" (via education, health, etc.) in ways capital has proven unwilling to do, but from which capitalists benefit extraordinarily.

Second, and even more important, relative autonomy allows the state to protect capitalism when capitalists themselves threaten to tear it apart. The state is the ideal institution *to protect capitalism from the capitalists*, who, when they each act on their own, tend to cause more than minor bumps in the market-mediated road. The state can legitimately coordinate and regulate their actions, and keep information on their actions in ways that the capitalists might hate, but that nonetheless are often the only reason the system works at all.

Keynesianism is perhaps the best example of a political economic analysis and associated set of policy recommendations premised upon the recognition that state capture by capital is not in capitalism's interest. Keynes (like Marx) believed capitalism was inherently crisis-prone due to the activities of capitalists (over-accumulation, underemployment, and so forth). The state's job in the Keynesian frame is to prevent or mitigate the effects of this volatility *so that capitalism will survive*. If the state did not enjoy some autonomy from capital, the capitalists would take it over and wreck everything, capitalism first of all. The state, as the "factor of cohesion" thus keeps capitalism running. It secures social peace via regulatory and legal mechanisms like monetary policy, redistributive tax systems, and property rights, thus giving capitalism legitimacy in the eyes of most people. Relative autonomy explains why and how it does so, and underlines the fact that there is no straightforward relation between capitalism and the democratic state. Things are far more complex than capitalist promises of "small government" and "free markets" suggest.

MONEY

Money in modern capitalism is inseparable from the state. An examination of how it works offers a fascinating and troubling perspective on contemporary liberal democracy and capitalist governance. Along with contracts and private property (see Chapter 4), money is perhaps *the* necessary precondition for capitalism. However, as with private property, this does not run both ways: you cannot have a capitalist economy that is nonmonetary, but you can certainly have a monetary economy that is noncapitalist. Money predates capitalism by thousands of years. The common assumption by both capitalists and contemporary economists that money is the supposedly "natural" response to the needs of exchange, and that these same needs lead just as "naturally" to capitalism, is completely unfounded.

Indeed, if money is the "natural" outcome of human economic development, then we would have to accept the absurd proposition that "traditional" nonmonetary societies—for example, the First Nations of the North American Pacific Northwest—are either "unnatural" (or they would have developed monetary economies) or developmentally "backward" (stalled on some universal and inevitable historical path). Neither proposition holds any water. English feudalism was no more "natural" than Northwest indigenous systems of tribute, slavery, and wealth distribution, and no particular trajectory of social or political economic change, in this case that of European capitalist societies, is universal and inevitable. Which is to say that money is not a "natural" institution, and when it does emerge, it does not necessarily lead to capitalism.

The true story of money is far more complex, as is the range of important roles it plays in capitalism. Not only is capitalism impossible without money, but money has functions in capitalism that help distinguish it from other monetized modes of production. First, money serves the necessary purpose of providing a stable measure of value, enabling the "trust" necessary for large-scale, impersonal economic relations. Second, stable money is the basis for an otherwise unimaginable range of creditor-debtor relations, to which few would willingly agree if they thought money would not have a reasonably similar value in the future. Without stable money values, relations like indenture, in which someone is contracted to labour for the creditor for a specified amount of time, would be far more common, because in that situation, it is immaterial if the bottom drops out of the value of money—the creditor still has the full "value" of his or her loan at hand in the form of unfree labour.

Because of the absolute centrality, then, of a stable measure of value widely accepted across time and space, all capitalist states are obsessed with maintaining a trusted and stable currency, and, in the modern era, with the protection of an integrated banking system through which money moves. Indeed, one of capitalism's distinguishing features is how readily relations of credit and debt are monetized, so readily it is hard for us to imagine them taking anything other than monetary form. But it is useful to remember that, like what the miller's daughter owed Rumpelstiltskin, it is not uncommon for debts to be redeemed in nonmonetary ways.

To see how this works, it is worth beginning even further back, with the question, What is money? This is much less straightforward than it appears. In standard introductory economics textbooks, money is commonly said to perform four functions: (1) It is a medium of exchange that facilitates the exchange of qualitatively different commodities. (2) It is a means of payment or transaction settlement, the thing with which you settle a debt, and usually legally defined as such. (3) It is a store of value; you can hold it as an asset in the form of abstract or potential purchasing power. (4) It is a unit of account; i.e., the standard unit by which all "economic" values are calculated and compared.[27]

---

27 These four functions are clearly closely related, and it is sometimes difficult to pry them apart. Functions (1) and (4), for example, might appear to be the same thing: isn't the fact that money is a standard unit of account the reason it is a medium of exchange, and vice versa? But in fact money can be one or other or both. It is not difficult to imagine a situation in which the medium of exchange is not standardized (as was the case

As I mentioned, classical and neoclassical economic analysis suggests that all of these functions flow from an original and primary function, (1) medium of exchange. In other words, it claims that money is first and foremost a convenience that helps solve the piano–fishing net problem referred to earlier. However, when examined in a more historically sensitive—and analytically adequate—manner, it is clear that as capitalism evolved, money became central primarily because of its key function as a standardized unit of account, which at least in capitalism is the most important role money plays. This role is not a product of the fact that it is some "thing" that circulates via exchange (currency or less "material" means of payment and settlement). Rather, as a unit of account it represents an abstract claim on or in circulation as a whole. Money measures and stores abstract purchasing power, and transports it through space and time. In a stable state system, in which standardization is associated with state sanction, you can use money "anywhere and anytime" (according to the territorial and customary restrictions associated with it). A Canadian dollar represents "abstract" (in the sense of yet to be specified) purchasing power exercisable, at least within Canada, at any place and time. It is the generalized unit of account for exchange in Canada: an "abstract" claim in the sense that as long as it is socially acceptable (to both buyer and seller), one can exercise that claim on

---

for much of history), and it is more than possible to have a standard unit of account that is not a medium of exchange. If commodities were accounted for according to the hours of labour in their production, and exchanged commodity-for-commodity on that basis, then we would have a unit of account that is not a medium of exchange.

assets in circulation by "spending" your money when and where you choose.

Money is the potential claim one may make upon the world of exchange. How does this work? You have to admit it is a remarkably powerful arrangement. Money rules the roost, but what social institutions and process-es endow it with this power? The easy answer is that we have collectively granted it this power, through implicit agreement. Even those of us skeptical of capitalism, who anticipate its dissolution in the not-too-distant future, readily and even eagerly accept money from our em-ployers (if we have one), and use it with the confidence capitalism requires. But this leaves the question of that "confidence" unaddressed, since we did not all get to-gether and come to some consensus on what this thing X is—money—and what it will do.

The best and most historically defensible expla-nation for money's astonishing power is that money is made to be what it is by a relationship between creditors and debtors denominated (quantitatively measured) in terms of an abstract unit of account. Money is produced by the contract between a borrower and lender, in which debt is "counted out" in a widely accepted unit of mea-sure. Money is "transferable" credit or debt insofar as it is issued as a claim upon the issuer in the creation of credit-debt contracts between two parties. The parties to these contracts are most commonly a bank and a bor-rower, the state and its contractors, the state and a bank, or the state and its citizens.

This is fairly complicated, so let's try to get a handle on it. When money is released into general circulation by a bank or a state, it is always issued via the process of debt creation. Which is to say, even though it is hard for many of us to believe, that much if not most of the money in circulation is produced when someone or some institution goes into debt. (Remember it need not be physical currency to circulate; currency represents a very small fraction of circulating money.) For example, when someone borrows money from a bank, it is not as if the bank has that money in bills and coins in a safe in the basement, nor does it have it in "digital" form. Instead, by lending money to the borrower (and thereby fulfilling its obligation to the debt contract), the bank basically "creates" that money. It simply creates a big hole in its own accounts, with a "minus" sign beside it. The debt contract stipulates that the borrower's obligation is to fill the hole by a set date. The money loaned does not need to pre-exist the debt contract. Which means that the debt contract literally creates the money, because the big hole the bank placed in its own accounts is mirrored by an equally large "pile" in the borrower's account. The borrower spends that money in the economy, and, in addition to the interest that is the price of using this money, slowly pays the bank back to fill the hole. The money produced via the loan is issued to the borrower who is then indebted, and the money represents the means of settling that debt.

The debt in this example is obviously private (between a borrower and a private bank), but money produced by the creation of their credit-debt contract can circulate generally in the public realm—if you borrow to pay your tuition, the money you borrow is not special money only you can use. Your school can use it to pay instructors and buy office furniture, instructors can use it to buy groceries, and so on. The money is a product of your indebtedness, and you can transfer it to whomever you please—it is transferable debt. Now, in theory, a bank cannot go on creating money in this way without limit. Modern banking systems have regulated "capital requirements": some portion of a bank's money-loan portfolio must be covered by reserves of cash or cash-like assets. But the ratio in most capitalist nation-states is only around 10 percent, often even less. Thus, at least in theory, unless all banks are simultaneously maxed out on their lending—unlikely, and even if it did happen, the banks merely have to go raise some more money to add to their reserves—the money supply can change size in response to demand for loans without direct state involvement.

Similarly, when the state creates money via spending, "printing," borrowing, etc., the money issued is a form of state debt. State-issued money is a claim on the state by the holder of the money, and it circulates among all the other private bank-issued debt-money: transferable debt. So, for example, when you come to settle your account with the state (pay your taxes, say), the state must accept its own credit-issue as legitimate means of redemption. The money is transferable debt that must be accepted as equivalent to the abstract unit of account.

As you might be wondering, the big question is why, with all these different contracts and parties involved, do we have only one kind of money per nation-state? That is a very good question. One of the definitive moments in capitalism's historical development was the point at which state-issued and bank-issued debt money became indistinguishable. Until very recently, debt-based money was specific to the lender in the contract: different banks issued their own money, the state had its money (and sometimes it used banks' or other states' money when it did not have enough of its own or could not exclude other moneys from circulating), and many firms had moneys ("scrip") with which they paid workers or issued credit. How did all these capitalist moneys fuse in the virtually unanimous acceptance of state-designated money as the universal unit of account? That they did is evidence of the institutional significance of money in modern capitalism, because the pace and extent of modern capitalist economic growth and development is not a cause, but a product of the integration of private currency (issued by banks) and sovereign debt (issued by states).

This fusion of moneys was a long and difficult process. It was made possible by the emergence in Europe of the balance of power between capital and the state discussed earlier, which Ingham (quoting Weber) calls the "memorable alliance." The state recognized the importance of a banking system that can create an elastic supply of credit-money in a self-generating process, fuelling economic growth. Capital recognized that that money could only enjoy the requisite confidence across space and time if it was secured by a strong territorial state. This essential alliance partly explains the complex interdependence of the capitalist state and its banking system, however fraught relations between capitalist states and finance capital might be these days.

THE CRUCIAL ROLE OF MONETARY AUTHORITY

In both capitalist and noncapitalist modes of production, any attempt to control monetary circulation is a complex and daunting task. But, given the centrality of the stable money to capitalism, control is necessary.

If money is allowed to increase in volume without restraint, inflation is likely, threatening the stability of money and the credit-debt contracts on which it is based. If all circulating money is used up to purchase all available goods and services, then any money added to the system will mean more money is now available for the purchase of the same amount of goods and services. In other words, every item for sale will cost more, so as to "use up" the extra money in circulation.

To avoid the problem of inflation induced by a growing money supply—too much money chasing too few goods—money in capitalism must be somewhat scarce. States have tried many different strategies for monetary governance, from commodity "standards" (which requires all money to be backed by a specified amount of some commodity, like gold; see Chapter 5), to officially abolishing old moneys when they have depreciated too much, and introducing new moneys (Germany annulled the mark after hyperinflation in the 1920s destroyed its value).

Today, capitalist money is "fiat" money. Its value is not based in a commodity like gold to which it can always be converted, but only in the state's guarantee. Since there is no longer a definitive limit on the amount of money available (which used to be constrained, for example, by the nation's gold reserves), monetary governance has become extremely complicated. In addition to regulations like banks' reserve requirements, the main arena of monetary policy in modern capitalism is so-called "money markets." Money markets—different than, but closely related to, capital markets for investment funds—coordinate the supply and demand for money. They are made up of interactions between the institutions involved in the credit-debt system: the state, the banks, and the central bank (which is managed, sometimes at considerable arm's length, by the state).

"Monetarism" is the name given to the influential but failed attempt on the part of neoclassically inspired monetary authorities, during the late 1970s and early 1980s, to control money markets—and therefore the value of money—from the supply side. The goal was to exercise authority over the capitalist economy by controlling the supply of money in circulation. It seemed straightforward, at least in theory. If the central bank can control the money supply, and its goal is to prevent inflation (or deflation) and keep prices stable, then all it needs to do is make sure the money supply and the range of goods and services it is chasing change at the same rate. That way, the price level should remain stable: if the economy grows by 2 percent in a year, then so should the money supply, and relative prices will stay basically the same. Monetarism flopped for both theoretical and practical reasons. It vastly underestimated how complicated a monetary economy actually is, and therefore came up with an economic model that was far too rigid, and based on enormously unrealistic assumptions. The state cannot precisely control monetary aggregates since, among other things, so much of the money in circulation is not state-issued, but created by private banks. Consequently, nobody could identify the right policy tool to change the "money supply" with any precision.

Contemporary monetary policy (since the late 1980s) is built on monetarist "supply-side" foundations, but it has abandoned the dream of using the money supply like a thermostat. Instead, through its central bank, the state tries to stimulate or constrain demand for money by manipulating prices in the money market using "interest rate operating procedures" (see Chapter 5). Interest rates are the price of money; when they are low, people tend to demand (borrow) more, and when they are high, people tend to demand (borrow) less. State participation in money markets through "open market operations" aims to establish a target rate of interest by influencing supply and demand. When the state wants to decrease interest rates, thus increasing the demand and supply of money, it typically purchases money market assets from financial institutions, which enlarges banks' cash reserves and allows them to expand their lending. When the state wants to increase interest rates to reduce the supply and demand for money, it sells assets on the money markets, which banks purchase, thereby reducing their reserves, constraining their lending.

Constant monetary policy fine-tuning is necessary—if interest rates stay too low for too long, so the theory goes, then the money supply will balloon and cause inflation; if it is too high for too long, borrowing for consumption and investment will dry up, and the economy will slow, perhaps even leading to deflation. Both have dire implications for capitalism because they represent a lack of stability in the unit of account. Inflation in its milder variations is not so bad—in fact, it can even help get a capitalist economy going. But hyperinflation, like that in Latin America in the 1980s, is a social disaster, as the real value of incomes and wealth plummets and life becomes a panicked attempt to spend money before it becomes valueless. Deflation, as the Great Depression taught us, is a downward spiral. Few will buy or invest when prices are falling.

What this means is that the capitalist battle against inflation and deflation is driven as much by political as economic imperatives. Monetary volatility affects both a state's internal stability and its geopolitical position in global capitalism. Moreover, monetary governance is not merely a tool to minimize collective or national hardship. It is also, at least as importantly, a force in domestic class politics, determining the very structure of the capitalist state. Recalling Poulantzas' point regarding the state as the "factor of cohesion" in capitalism, we know that conflicts at the heart of capitalist resource distribution include not only "classic" struggles between labour and capital, but also conflicts between "civil society" and the state, among capitalists themselves, and among different groups of workers. And monetary authority is an oft-forgotten but crucial site of these struggles, especially between various fractions of capital.

Money is the blood of capital's body, and monetary authority is a key to power in modern capitalism. This is partly because the ways in which banks and states create money produces intense conflict between debtors and creditors (remember that many debtors are capitalists, both individuals and firms). The price of money (the interest rate) is enormously important to both borrowers and lenders, and unlike some other markets, the state plays a decisive role in determining it, by setting the base interest rates for the whole economy. So winning over the state to one's cause—cheap money if one owes, dear money if one is owed—is a high-stakes political fight, in the most straightforward meaning of "political."

One of the better known fronts in this battle is that waged on and off by North American farmers since the mid-nineteenth century. It began with the Grange and

Greenback movements in the US, in what is commonly known as Populism, and in the emergence of the Co-operative Commonwealth Federation in western Canada—the first incarnation of what is now called the New Democratic Party. It persists today in small business and farm lobbies.[28] The fundamental issue in these struggles is farmers' debts, which have always been enormous, and tend to be more burdensome the smaller the operation. Given the relationship between the money supply and inflation, farmers have generally favoured monetary expansion, since this should in theory lower interest rates and make it cheaper to repay loans. In the nineteenth century, when many capitalist countries operated on a gold standard, farmers all over the capitalist world demanded—but rarely received—a "bimetallic" standard, with silver also counting as a basis for monetary issue, so the money supply could increase and their debts diminish. This is what the US Populist presidential candidate William Jennings Bryan meant when he said, in what is surely the most famous speech given by a US presidential candidate who did not win, "We will not be crucified on a cross of gold." This is a political struggle at the heart of what today would be called the "money markets," and it unfolds less between workers and capitalists fighting over the surplus than between different capitalist firms fighting over how and for whom markets will work.

---

28 The "farm lobbies" are no longer closely associated with what most people imagine when they think of a "farmer," but with some of the biggest and most powerful industrial corporations in the world, in whose hands much of the future of the global food supply now rests: Con-Agra, Archer Daniels Midland, Monsanto, Cargill, Syngenta, etc.

4

Markets, Contracts, and Firms

In this second chapter on capitalist institutions, I try to integrate a discussion of markets and firms in capitalism, and the contractual relationships upon which both depend. Contracts establish, with the sanction of the state, the legal and property relations that are essential to markets and firms, and to all individuals and groups in capitalism, including the state itself. It is almost impossible to exaggerate the importance of contracts to capitalism, and to its political legitimacy. Contracts are how private property "actually operates" in capitalism. To start, however, let's turn to a few crucial preliminaries.

"THE" MARKET?

In capitalism, the market is often treated like one of the fundamental forces of the universe, as independent of human desires as gravity. This deified market is obviously mythical, but the myth did not arise without reason. Markets really are central to the operation of capitalism, the first mode of production in history in which the market is *the* principal means of coordination. The principal, however, does not mean the only: the idea that markets determine all resource allocation in capitalism is categorically false. "Nonmarket" influences like coercion, tribute, and command still matter a great deal—especially within the firm, and often in the family (which remains an important institution of social reproduction in capitalism). Markets are nevertheless the main means of coordination and allocation in the capitalist world today; where widespread subsistence production has disappeared, markets are the principal way people meet their basic (and nonbasic) needs. Very few people in the global North today can provide for themselves the shelter, food, and water necessary to survive without engaging in market transactions—and those who can often choose to use markets anyway. Even for those of us radically opposed to it, living in a society organized by capital makes it very difficult to avoid market participation.

This, in fact, is one of Marx's principal historical conclusions: if markets are the way things get distributed, and you do not have access to the means of production yourself, then you must purchase your subsistence on the market. However, because capitalist markets are fully monetized—you cannot walk into 7-11 and barter for a carton of milk—participation is restricted to those with money. Since most of us can only access the means of production, and thus a way of making a living, by selling our labour-power to a capitalist, we have no choice but to enter the labour market to obtain the money with which we pay rent, buy groceries, feed and clothe the family, etc. Getting by in capitalism, in the material if not the emotional sense, is almost entirely a market-mediated experience, even for those who curse the thought. This vicious cycle is a big part of the reason many people see few options other than shutting up and doing their jobs—an imperative that only grows in force as opportunities for paid work decline in "tough times," and the fear of unemployment disciplines us more harshly.

Abolishing or finding a way out of this "wage-worker's bind" is one of the most significant challenges for anticapitalist politics. Millions, even billions, of people all over the world today feel trapped in their current capital-imposed position, quite reasonably terrified of rejecting it, since as it stands there is no other way to put food on their table and keep a roof over their children's heads. This is precisely what Marx described with bitter irony as the condition of the "free worker" in capitalism. Any successful anticapitalism must both explain and upend the forces that produce the wage-worker's bind, *and* make a compelling case for how a better getting by will be possible when existing structures are no longer standing. Indeed, making arguments like this is a big part of what "politics" is.

Making that case will be difficult, but not impossible. A first step is to expose the myth that we are beholden to impersonal market forces that no one really controls. Contrary to the impression one gets from the media, just because the market is essential to capitalism, does not mean that capitalism *is* the market. That it appears to be is a crucial thread in the wage-worker's bind. In truth, markets are only part of the capitalist system, a substantial and essential part to be sure, but there are others: state, firm, family, nonmarket institutions like community groups and teams, and so forth. Nor are markets neutral realms in which supply and demand coolly intersect via the logic of competitive prices, as the harmonious classical and neoclassical models suggest.

Markets are principal sites of conflict in capitalism, usually between actors who are not themselves organized according to market logic. If you think about it, even though the capitalist enterprise, the family (however defined), the state, and workers' organizations are among the key participants in capitalist markets, and some of them (especially firms and the state) are the loudest proponents of the benefits of market organization, not one is internally organized according to market principles. Internal relations in firms are not determined by atomistic competition any more than internal distribution of incomes in the civil service are determined by individual marginal contribution to productivity.

The internal structure of most "capitalist" organizations is proof that capitalism is not only not the same as the market, but that much of capitalism is constituted in, and depends upon, a vast array of nonmarket institutions and relations. Virtually all capitalist firms have a command structure much more like the military than the market, and families have a whole range of structures, even within one society. The state is a massive and often uncoordinated mess of different interests and actors—nominally pyramid-like but in reality many little pyramids—and unions are never, as far as I know, structured by market principles. Despite what you might expect, not all orthodox economists have ignored these nonmarket forces. Many working in the field of institutional (or "new institutional") economics have struggled to understand them, because according to their assumptions about human motivation, willing participation in nonmarket relations only makes sense if it provides access to benefits that capitalist markets, by definition, should be better at providing.

That the main theoreticians of what we might call "capitalist reason" recognize the importance of nonmarket spaces is not academic trivia: their ideas can help us understand institutions anticapitalists sometimes confuse as safe havens from the power of capital. These scientists of capitalist reason—today found mainly in economics and political science departments at the most influential universities in the global North, and in the international institutions whose managers they train (the International Monetary Fund, the World Bank, the World Trade Organization, and finance ministries and central banks)—have formulated increasingly sophisticated ways of understanding nonmarket institutional foundations, and of using and shaping them in capital's interest. They know, for example, that many migrant workers could never survive on what they get paid, but they also know that a significant portion of them rely in some way on family-based forms of subsistence, so they can be paid less than if they were fully market-dependent. This means that some common staples of "left" critique are questionable. On one hand, it means capital is not necessarily always interested in the destruction of communities, although it may of course have an interest in destroying a particular community, like that of an indigenous people whose territory sits atop oil and gas deposits. On the other hand, it also means that subsistence-based communities do not necessarily offer an escape from the power of capital. They might, but that potential cannot reside merely in the fact that they are not market-based or fully monetized. There has to be something more specific to a community and its relations to capitalist markets, firms, and states to ensure freedom from the dictates of capital.

Relations between market-organized and nonmarket aspects of capitalism are complex, subject to the imperative to accumulate and to the specific histories and cultures, and sometimes even the individuals, in question. People come to the market, as a realm of social interaction, with widely varying degrees of power to shape the relationships that make up the market. The laissez-faire claim that prices and distribution are determined via neutral exchange between equals is poppycock.

Economists are not entirely blind to this, of course, although they tend to emphasize only the most blatant violations of the "law of one price" associated with monopoly and other forms of "market power" or "price discrimination."[29] "Market power" is an umbrella term describing the capacity of any market actor to influence market dynamics in their favour. Orthodox analysts, like the rest of us, recognize that market power is ubiquitous, but, since it is assumed to be impossible in perfectly functioning markets (because perfect competition between many buyers and sellers prevents any one agent from affecting the equilibrium price), there is a special term for it. "Price discrimination" is one way a market participant can exercise market power. It means having the power to buy or sell at a "special," nonequilibrium price. This dynamic operates throughout contemporary capitalism. For example, if only a few large corporations produce a commodity in high demand—personal computers or gasoline, say—then competition will not necessarily drive prices down, because the producers can de-

---

29 The "law of one price" states that in perfect markets, where all participants are "price takers" with all relevant information, the price for any particular commodity will be the same in all markets.

velop a pricing "norm" that is not too close to the bone. They don't even have to do this illicitly, via collusion or "price-fixing"; the general rate of profit can evolve as a tacit understanding, around which minor innovations in quality or production costs create slight movements, but no drastic change in consumer prices. This market structure may even drive prices up, since in markets for luxury and high-price goods, consumers frequently will buy a more expensive item because they assume its price accurately indicates its quality. Corporations like Apple understand this very well. There is a reason why, when you hear of a $100 laptop, it never turns out to be an Apple or an IBM product.

Take another, better-known example, one many of us have seen in our neighbourhoods. If Walmart wants to crush local competition (which it does), it can price some goods below cost and handle the temporary losses because it is so big. In the lingo, Walmart is a "price-maker." Since smaller operators cannot compete with these prices for more than brief periods (they are "price-takers"), and they have less size and capital to fall back on, they eventually shut their doors. At that point, Walmart usually raises its prices back up to highly profitable levels, confident in its new monopoly. When I was living in Guelph, Ontario, in the mid-1990s, I witnessed a particularly nefarious version of this. At that time, Guelph was still a mostly non-"box store," down-town-business kind of place, perhaps because it was surrounded by land zoned, and used, for agriculture. Its city council refused to approve a massive Walmart on the edge of town. So, Walmart purchased empty retail space on the main street and opened under the name of "Bargain! Bargain! Bargain!" (I could not make that up.)

It proceeded with the standard discriminatory pricing practice its market power affords, killed off local competitors, and when it finally wore down resistance to the box store, it shut its doors and opened a monster on the edge of town, leaving downtown to rot.

This story exemplifies a larger process of which Walmart is only a part. Many argue that contemporary capitalism is increasingly characterized by so-called "monopolistic competition" between a limited number of very large players. This is indeed the norm in many sectors and markets, not just box-store retailing. Monopolistic competition persists because of market power and significant "barriers to entry" in many industries. It is difficult to get in on the action because you need a lot of money or land or connections, and there are many ways existing firms secure control of the market. The banking and oil industries are classic examples; it is basically impossible to go out and start your own bank or oil company.

As these dynamics suggest, prices are ultimately the product of a whole range of relations that includes, but is in no way limited to, competition. It is probably better described as a struggle—this is obvious with wages (the price of labour-power)—that introduces considerable uncertainty and instability into capitalism. However, while economists pay more attention to uncertainty and (limited) instability these days, much of modern economic theory continues to assume, for purposes of analysis if not its practical implementation, that markets are "perfect": it assumes that everyone is a "price-taker," that prices are instantly and infinitely flexible, that participants have all necessary information about present and future prices, and that everyone will act "rationally"

to optimize their self-interest or utility according to preferences that are entirely determined *outside* the market.
This last is essential to orthodox theories of capitalism,
but it is particularly bewildering, given how central the
market god is to their account of social life. It means that
the neoclassical or market-centred theory of value and
distribution paradoxically asserts that market relations
have no effect on your likes, desires, or needs; for the theory to work, these must be determined "somewhere else."

To say "perfect" markets are purely mythical seems
like stating the obvious. But I mean it in two precise
ways. First, they are mythical in the straightforward
sense that they can never exist outside the imagination—as mythical as Hercules cleaning the dung out of
Augeus' stables by diverting two rivers. This is no surprise to noneconomists among us. But, contrary to a
common (and misleading) anticapitalist criticism, it is
no surprise to economists either. Orthodox economists
do not walk the Earth naïvely believing all markets are
actually perfect, if only the rest of us could see it. They
know full well they are not. But orthodox capitalist analysts do not assume perfection because it accurately
represents the world, but rather because without it, the
formal modeling they do is impossible.[30]

---

30 I think it worth stressing the adjective "formal" here, as opposed to the common description of modern economics as
"mathematical" or "quantitative," It is true that some fields of
economic study—especially statistics-driven econometrics—
are very mathematical or quantitative in this sense. But modern
economic theory, which at first glance looks very mathematical, is more often than not using symbols to describe qualitative relations. Readers of contemporary economic theory rarely
see actual numbers. It is all about formal abstraction via symbols. The real numerical "values" are not the point.

Second, and to my mind more significant, perfect markets are mythical in the Utopian sense. They are not only a dream, they are an ideal to which we are supposed to aspire, a model we are told we should emulate. Modern economic theory is "performative"—a fancy way of saying it purports to describe a situation that it is in fact trying to produce—and in that sense, the perfect market of neoclassical Assumptionland stands today as the standard by which actual markets are judged; it is the perfect 10 of efficiency, productivity, and neutrality. This is the principal justification for opposition to any regulation, stipulation, or social barrier that represents a reduction in the "freedom" of markets to operate "unfettered": they make it impossible to get to the promised land.

One of the biggest problems with this myth is that since the assumptions that make it possible can never be realized (we can never have perfect foresight or respond to market shifts instantaneously) it is unclear if the maximizing, efficiency, and utilitarian welfare claims can *ever* be realized. Even on modern theories' own terms, markets will only perform all their supposed magic— optimize individual and collective welfare efficiently—if the assumptions hold. If they don't (and we know they don't), then if is not clear what markets can and cannot actually do. It is no exaggeration to say we have no evidence to suggest that "more" perfect markets are worth pursuing. The faith that tacitly underwrites orthodox wisdom—although, as far as I know, never stated explicitly—is that the "perfection" of markets is a sort of "the closer the better" intuition. The closer the market to mythical perfection, the more efficiency, productivity, and neutrality we should expect to enjoy. There is an implicit assumption that there are no "threshold" effects at work, that the "perfect market" is not an all-or-nothing affair, but something we can aim at, like the bull's-eye on a target. If we hit close to the mark, well then that is better than being far away, right?

But what if, even if we adopt the orthodox faith that markets can in principle do all this fantastic work, the benefits provided by "perfect" markets *are* an all-or-nothing thing? If so, it is bad news for capitalist reason, because we know for certain that the "all" option—100 percent perfect market—is impossible. In the economics profession, the modeling that formulates the as-near-as-possible-to-perfection argument involves a sort of staged analysis. It begins with a set of propositions about the dynamics of interest in an assumed "perfect" market. Next, some of these assumptions are "relaxed," so the model more closely approximates the "real world." For example, to model the effect of an unexpected shift in the supply of oil, the first step would be a bare bones model constructed assuming perfect markets, fully formed and perfectly ordered preferences, etc., from which basic relationships can be constructed. In subsequent steps, restrictive assumptions—say, the assumption that all the world's oil supply is equally and instantaneously available—are relaxed, to yield a more "realistic" picture. Usually, this means the models get more and more complicated as the analysis unfolds, since they need more variables to take account of real-world complexities, like geographical barriers to some oil supplies.

But this process builds two potentially fatal weaknesses into the argument derived from the model. First, the more "realistic" conclusions, formulated with relaxed assumptions, are still built upon the infrastructure of a mythical market Utopia. The "real world" is posited as a second-rate variation (the technical term is "second-best") on an *a priori* ideal. Its dynamics are always a flawed version of those at work in Assumptionland. The real world is never taken in its own actuality as the basis for understanding. Yet the real world is all we ever have—and the real world *is* imperfection. Perfection— in markets or anything else—is not some deep-lying or transcendent feature we have to uncover or attain. It is not there *at all, anywhere.*

Second, the only way modeling can handle the "real world" features that emerge when assumptions are relaxed is to incorporate them as variables. But variables are only useful for representing things that are, at least in theory, measurable. I do not mean to say that variables are useless. The common claim that economics is evil because it "quantifies" everything is a weak and distracting argument; too many radical critics give it too much emphasis. It is hard to imagine that whatever world anticapitalism produces will not require lots of "quantitative" analysis. The very notion of redistribution—central to any anticapitalist politics—is unavoidably, if not completely, quantitative. My point is that the only assumptions modelers can relax are those that define "market perfection." They cannot, therefore, take into account either the necessary but by no means stable nonmarket dynamics that undergird "perfection"—social peace, the language mix, the politics of gender, noncatastrophic weather, for example—or market dynamics that are resistant to measurement, like "expectations."[31]

---

31 Expectations play a crucial part of modern economics, but there is still no way to directly measure them. Models use some "proxy" that is measurable, like the price difference between bonds of different maturities, or assume that everyone expects

Orthodox arguments about what markets can do only understand the "market" dimensions of markets, and can only understand those relative to a mythical standard. They cannot comprehend markets as dynamic social institutions, embedded, sometimes deeply, sometimes precariously, in real times and places. They cannot comprehend politics as anything other than external "disturbance" of the market, an obstacle to perfection.

Ultimately, orthodoxy does not have a very strong argument for the superiority of market organization, in the sense that it cannot base it on any sort of proof or logic. On the contrary, the commitment to the market is more a leap of faith; a leap, we are told, that if we all take it together, will performatively make it so. The fact that many of us are reluctant to take the leap has paradoxically become one of the go-to excuses for the failure of markets to work their magic. When capitalism does not deliver the goods, free marketeers almost inevitably attribute it to the fact that we are not committed enough to the market, that somehow we still intervene, preventing competition from realizing its potential.

It should be noted that the economic justification for capitalist markets I have criticized over the last several pages is a particularly rigid variety. It has several names and manifestations, but at its strictest it is labeled "Chicago School" economics, because much of its argumentative and technical power was developed at the University of Chicago's economics department. Many people I know, after reading books like Naomi Klein's *Shock Doctrine*, are under the impression that since Keynesianism fell out of favour in the early 1970s, all

---

the future to be like the past or the present—which just sweeps the problem under the rug.

economics is Chicago economics, which is not so. While modern economics, at least in its neoclassical varieties, is heavily influenced by Chicago-style thinking, not all neoclassical economists are the same, and not all neo-classical economists justify markets the same way. This is important because it means that the capitalist case for market-organized society is not entirely undone by the failures of classical and neoclassical mythology. There is, for example, a relatively influential "Austrian" per-spective whose most famous advocate is Friedrich von Hayek, maybe the most famous free marketeer outside of Adam Smith and Milton Friedman (the high priest of Chicago).

Hayek and the Austrians argue that markets are the optimal institutions for coordinating social life for rea-sons very different from the Chicago Schoolers. They say (as I have) that perfect markets assume impossible cogni-tive capacities for calculation, foresight, and information organization. No one—no person, no firm, no institu-tion, no state—can handle all that knowledge, even if it were available. According to the Austrian tradition, mar-kets are good not because they approximate perfection, but because they deal with uncertainty and change better than other ways of allocating resources and disseminat-ing information. A lot of this is because they "distribute," or "decentralize," knowledge and decision-making power to market participants. This flexibility allows them to or-ganize people, things, and information in ways that suits their needs, and to innovate in ways that centralized co-ordination and resource allocation generally inhibit.

Chicago School orthodoxy is often targeted by the anticapitalist left, especially in the superficial "you can't quantify love" way, because it is an easy target for ridicule. When Hayek comes up at all in critical accounts, he is almost always lumped in with Chicago-style thinking. But the Austrian critique is sharp, and makes a lot of sense. It is far more important that critics of capitalism engage this argument for "free" markets than that of classical or neoclassical orthodoxy, not least because it is much more compelling. It also shares certain features with a radical analysis in its focus on the limits of the state and formal institutions, and it is no accident that Hayek is often associated with a libertarianism not always very far from some varieties of anarchism.

Given some of the more terrifyingly disastrous experiments in "planning" and non-market-based modes of social organization that cloud twentieth-century history—Stalinism, Maoism, etc.—there seems to be *very* good reason to believe that even a well-meaning "coordinator" of economic life is doomed to fail. Not only were these episodes devastating political and economic calamities, but the vast majority who bore the costs, millions of them with their lives, were those at the bottom of the socioeconomic ladder, precisely those with whom anticapitalism is most concerned. If anticapitalist goals demand a renewed energy for planning—something far more likely than I believe many of us are willing to admit, and which should not be undertaken lightly—then it must struggle mightily with the problem posed by the Austrian analysis, which defends markets not because they might be perfectly efficient, but because their imperfections are preferable to a coerced, nonmarket "perfection." It is worth remembering that Hayek wrote not to propose some capitalist dream come true, but to provide an antidote to totalitarianism and fascism—two tendencies we still need to be vigilant to avoid.

WHAT MARKETS CAN AND CANNOT DO

With this in mind, let us turn to a more specific analysis of markets in actually existing capitalism. There are in fact many different markets, and many different kinds of markets, the relations between which vary a great deal. Sometimes markets overlap, sometimes they intersect occasionally, and sometimes they are almost completely distinct. Examples include money markets like those discussed in Chapter 3, financial asset markets, labour markets, and producer markets (both for intermediate goods that firms buy for production purposes, and for consumers purchasing "final" goods). There are also hybrids, like carbon offsets or pollution permits markets, which are a little harder to place in more conventional categories.

However we conceive of markets, though, there are situations in which they don't seem to work all that well—and not merely relative to the perfection some assume they should attain, but even relative to suitably diminished "real-world" expectations. Economists call these "market failures," and perhaps the most commonly noted is the case of so-called "public goods." In political economy, public goods are not just things that are good for the public, but goods or services that it helps everyone to have, but for which there is insufficient incentive for capitalist investment. Think about air quality, for example. Clearly, clean air is something everyone wants, and from which everyone benefits. But even if an entrepreneur could come up with a way of "cleaning" the air, there is no way he or she could make a return on their investment because it would be impossible to prevent people from breathing cleaned air for free. Clean air, at least so far, is what economists call "nonexcludable" and "nonrival"—you may be able to provide it for a price, but it is impossible to prevent someone from using it at no cost (nonexcludability), and no matter how much one person uses, it does not diminish available supplies (nonrivalry). In the case of clean air, then, there is no market incentive to provide it: you can't exclude those who don't pay from using it, and no matter who or how many uses it, there is always enough left for others. In other words, you can't control its distribution via contract and you can't make it scarce enough to merit a price.

Orthodox economists consider the failure to provide public goods a "market failure," and it is one instance in which many of them endorse the state as the logical provider. Even Adam Smith listed public goods like infrastructure as part of the state's necessary tasks in capitalism.

Other market failures have little or nothing to do with the nature of the goods or services in question. Monopoly is, as we noted earlier, a common problem, usually viewed by economists and policy-makers as a market failure. Because monopolistic firms are not price-takers—participation is not broad or deep enough to prevent some from exercising market power—markets don't do their job well, at least as that job is described by neoclassical or Austrian theory. This is because economic power in capitalism becomes highly concentrated, a developmental pattern it has never escaped. Which suggests that it is less a "failure" of capitalist markets than an almost universal tendency. Again, the frame of analysis—a mythical Utopian standard of perfection by which actually existing economic and social relations are judged—determines the conclusion. Rather than delineating the limits of markets' utility, and therefore the realms in which they are socially inappropriate, what capitalist markets cannot do is defined as a "failure"—relative to an impossible dream.

Another important problem in marketized relations of all sorts is a condition economists have given the ugly name of "asymmetric information." This is the basically universal situation in which one party in a contract has some meaningful information not available to the other party—usually called the "counterparty" (a term that says so much so succinctly). This asymmetry in knowledge builds uncertainty, complexity, and contingency into virtually all contracts, dynamics that usually increase in importance the longer the term of the contract and the further the geographical distance between the parties. For example, if a firm in Germany contracts a factory in my home of Vancouver (Canada) to produce something, one of the main things on the German firm's mind will be making sure that they are not getting ripped off, and that the Canadian firm is doing a good job. If they sign a long-term contract, the risks only get bigger, because if they are getting taken for a ride, or if the product is of lower-than-expected quality, they are trapped in the relationship for a long time. Also, the fact that the factory is thousands of miles away will worry them. It is not as if management can just drop by to check in on the way home from work. Consequently, the German firm will almost certainly try to write a contract to take account of these concerns, perhaps including opt-out clauses if quality drops below a certain level, or if competitors drop their prices a certain amount, etc. All these bits and pieces of the contract are part of the German firm's attempt to manage the fact that on these questions—quality, timing, cost, etc.—the people at the Canadian factory know far more than them. The distribution of information is "asymmetric."

Some of the most influential ideas concerning these problems are the focus of the subfield of "economics of information" (Obama advisor, Nobel Prize-winner, and former World Bank chief economist Joseph Stiglitz is its best known practitioner), and of the new institutional economics mentioned earlier. Together, they constitute a kind of hybrid of neoclassical market-clearing ideas and Keynesian uncertainty. These economists commonly frame challenges to market function like asymmetric information as "principal-agent" problems: the principal is the contractor and the agent is the "contractee," the person or firm hired to do the work. In every such two-party ("bilateral") contract, one party is usually asked to do something (build a boat, work at the factory, provide information, or care for a sick patient) and one party requests the service, goods, or information. The doer is the "agent" in the relationship, the asker or hirer is the "principal." As in any other social interaction, it is likely that one party to the contract has access to information that the other does not. Usually, this is understood as a problem for the principal, i.e., information asymmetry favours the agent.

There are countless examples of this in everyday contracts. Imagine I hire you to build a boat, with agreed-upon material and labour costs. I am the principal. Now suppose that you, the builder (agent), find a cheaper supply of timber or fittings than you anticipated. Will you tell me, and reduce the price of the boat? I am a fisherman; I have no access to the people and suppliers you do, I have little knowledge of what constitutes a "normal" price for timber or fittings, and I have no networks with which to find a "good deal" on these supplies. Alternatively, imagine that the state hires my firm to deliver the mail, for which I hire individual carriers. Since recipients of mail rarely know if or when they will receive it, it is difficult for the state, or my firm, to know if I am adequately fulfilling my contractual obligations. Carriers could just pile the mail up in their apartment each day. Monitoring their work, my speed, etc., is very difficult for the state, and my firm has little incentive to do so (I am being paid by the state anyway). As contracts accumulate, the principal-agent problems become complicated; the state is a principal, the carrier and I are both agent and principal; and the recipient, whose taxes fund postal services, is also a principal.

For capital, such problems can become extremely complex with big-money, long-term contractual arrangements, like labour recruiting or supply-chain management. If I hire you to set up my factory overseas, for which I pay the construction costs, how do I ensure you are seeking the best deal or best-quality workers, firms, materials, and sites? How can I know you will ensure maximum efficiency in construction, if you are not responsible for, or may even benefit from, cost and timeline overruns? That you are being careful not to (blatantly) violate environmental or human rights laws, for which I might get pilloried on the front pages in five years? These principal-agent concerns upset the supposedly competitive market price determination process, and the most common solution to them are explicitly non-market-based, noncompetitive arrangements: cost-sharing deals, independent subsidiaries that free firms from legal obligations, time-sensitive contracting, security forces to watch workers work. Sometimes, one party might even purchase the other firm, eliminating the market mediation of the relationship, and moving the agent inside the nonmarket command hierarchy of the principal.

Institutional economics has long been interested in this last option, what is commonly described as the firm's choice between "markets" or "hierarchies." In every transaction, the capitalist firm decides whether to do something in-house or to obtain the same goods or services on the market, by subcontracting, purchasing, etc. To go outside of the firm is to choose markets, to keep it in the firm is to choose hierarchies. The idea is that markets may not be able to solve coordination, information, and efficiency problems, as neo/classical theory claims. These other informational and transactional concerns sometimes mean it is better, although not necessarily cheaper, to keep it in-house.

Despite the either/or framing, in capitalism the realms of market and the firm are in fact necessary complements. There is choice regarding markets and hierarchies because both are essential to capitalist relations of production, distribution, and consumption. It is not like capitalism can only have one or the other. In fact—and this is crucial to an examination of modern capitalism—the capitalist firm is a response to the information, coordination, and social conditions that limit what markets can do. In other words, one of the fundamental institutions of capitalism exists precisely because orthodox economics is wrong, and markets cannot do the work they are supposed to do.

Here, we are looking beyond "microeconomic" or firm-scale decisions with respect to contractual "counterparties" and more at capitalism's "macro" social institutions and relations, which dominate and determine the limits of the micro. At a similar macro-scale, contractual relations between individuals, firms, and other actors (the state, for instance) in capitalism are determined by the inequalities that differentiate market participants. It is not just firms that vary in market power—different social groups and classes come to the market on unequal footing. The structural advantage enjoyed by capital in the labour market, especially in the "neoliberal" era, is a clear example (see Chapter 6). There is an even greater power asymmetry between labour and capital inside the firm, because the composition and level of demand for labour is largely determined by capital. It decides, almost unilaterally, the how much, who, and where of wage work, while supply, as we know from earlier discussions, is not a choice for most workers. The wage-worker's bind means they have to supply labour to get by.

The conflict here is necessarily entangled in the larger conflict over the distribution of surplus and social power in economic activity. That conflict impinges upon virtually all markets and enterprises because it concerns the most common contract in capitalism: the employment contract. Workers sell labour-power to firms, but labour-power is not like other commodities. Buyers of other commodities can separate them from the producer. But when you are hired for wages, you—your person, your will, your politics, your energy, and so on—come with the commodity, irreducibly bound to it. It is not nearly as easy for the firm to determine the disposition of the commodity—the worker's time and energy.

This problem is most notable in struggles over the labour process—the ways daily work is organized. The classic example is the "factory floor," but any workplace has similar issues. Workers and capital have long fought over the content and form of work: capitalist specialization and division of labour; mechanization and deskilling (so-called "Taylorism"), and the end of, and nostalgia for, craft work; the Fordist "compromise" or Great Accord between big labour, big business, and big government that lasted for a quarter-century after World War II (see Chapter 5). Labour process is the object of some of workers' most effective resistance tactics, like strikes or work-to-rule struggles.

Large-scale and incredibly complex problems also arise over regulation in capitalism. This is, in fact, one of the classic real-world challenges that spurred the study of contracts and information. For almost all regulation—environmental, economic, electoral, and so on—the regulator, as principal, is at a massive disadvantage. They may have the heavy hand of the state on their side, but monitoring behaviour across an enormous range of tasks, firms, environments, territory, and activity is never easy. In environmental regulation alone—something that concerns even those opposed to the state—the cost of adequately monitoring capitalist environmental impacts would be staggering (this is not the only reason we don't do it, unfortunately). Imagine trying to ensure all mining corporations respected groundwater protections or timber companies adhered to stream-buffer regulations during harvest. The troubling truth is that in most capitalist nation-states, the regulator's information concerning firm behaviour comes mostly from the firm itself. This is a very real, and very big, problem, and while it is particularly evident in geographically remote resource extraction, it is also a problem in more "fixed" sectors, like banking or telecommunications.

As the recent financial crisis demonstrates, firms need not operate in a roadless Arctic tundra to lie beyond the eye of the regulator and the public. The organizational technical complexity of many industries has reached a point, and changes so rapidly, that it is impossible for regulators to keep up. In fact, it is often difficult for regulators to even understand what is going on, or, if they do, to determine if it falls under existing regulations, or if it is so new it does not fit at all.

Take the financial sector. As most of us have now learned, the financial crisis that began in 2007 was triggered by the collapse of a vast pool of "securitized" mortgages in the US. And, as most of us have heard, these securities were incredibly "complicated," produced by the technical and mathematical genius of "financial innovation." Both claims are debatable (that they were complicated or that geniuses were involved), as is whether securitization was really where the most important dynamics were at work. But there is no denying that from a computational perspective, securitization has become almost overwhelming. The technical modeling through which new securities are created or derived from other financial assets (hence the blanket term "derivatives"), and how their prices are determined, often requires years of training in financial economics or computer science. Almost all the people with those skills work for the firms, not for government, and even if the state manages to hire a few of them—inevitably paid much less—there aren't enough to go around. Since the firms are doing all the "innovating" via fancy mathematics and contractual design, it is very hard for the state to avoid a level of "asymmetric information" that forces the regulator (the principal) to simply accept the firm's (the agent's) assurance that everything is under control, and all important risks are understood and accounted for. That is precisely what Goldman Sachs and Bear Stearns and the rest of the most powerful perpetrators of the crisis assured the financial authorities over and over—then, boom! Up in smoke went the credit market, and with it much of the global economy.

Obviously finance is not the only sector we can characterize in these terms. Regulating biotechnology, for example, entails similar challenges. Biotech firms create new genes and seeds with state-of-the-art knowledge and technique, and then report to the state what they have done. Regulating agencies hopefully do their utmost to understand what new seeds or genes can do, how they work, and what risks they pose. But that is not easy, even with the expertise to understand the process. With few exceptions, after a few tests, the regulator says "be careful," and hopes it all works out. This is to say nothing of the common problem of "regulatory capture" in capitalist (and noncapitalist) states. In innovation-driven sectors like biotech, pharmaceuticals, energy, and finance, the very same people doing the regulating have often worked for, and have close personal and professional ties to, the firms they oversee. The well-documented "revolving door" between regulating agencies and firms means that regulators are for all intents and purposes colleagues of those they are supposed to monitor.[32] The fact that Hank Paulson, former head of Goldman Sachs, was the US secretary of the treasury—for both Bush Jr. and Obama—says it all.

---

32 See "Regulator Capture, A Case Study," *Financial Times*, 29 June 2012.

Just as workers might slack off if they are not being watched, capitalist "cheating" limits effective regulation. Firms will often ignore, break, or lobby against any rule that limits profitability—witness the 2012 revelation that big banks have been profitably manipulating the most important interest rate in the world (LIBOR, the London Interbank Offered Rate) for years.[33] However, many serious regulatory problems arise not only because firms behave "opportunistically," breaking rules when violations are not immediately observable, like looking over both shoulders and then dumping the recycling in the trash can. Further limits to what regulation can and do originate in complicated, "structural" ways that are not addressed simply by putting more inspectors on the ground or demanding more frequent reporting.

For example, in media coverage of the recent financial crisis, you may have come across the problem of "moral hazard." This term describes how, with certain kinds of contracts (including "implicit" contracts like that between a regulator and a regulated firm), the agent might not exercise due caution because, if things go awry, the cost of risky or ill-conceived action will be borne all or in part by the principal. The classic case of moral hazard is capitalist insurance markets. We have all heard of someone intentionally burning down their house or factory for the insurance money. I have no idea how often that actually happens, but the fact that the insured (the agents) might act that way is of great concern to insurers (the principals), and creates all sorts of contractual and pricing complexities that prevent markets from finding an equilibrium price and clearing. It is also how insurers justify how expensive their services

---

33 *Financial Times*, 24 July 2012.

are: since principals have a hard time identifying a "really" trustworthy agent, they charge everybody more.

Moral hazard becomes extremely significant when the principal is the "people" or "citizenry," as represented in the capitalist state.[34] If the state, in its modern guise as the institutional manifestation of the principal's authority, has to bear some or all the costs associated with firms' malfeasance—as it readily did during the financial crisis—it is the public who bears the costs. When states bailed out banks and other financial firms that had taken seemingly crazy risks with their assets and those of others, those states were potentially making the next crisis even worse by increasing the risk of moral hazard on the part of banks and finance capital in general. By making it clear the state would help clean up the mess, the state essentially assured the firms that it was acceptable to take risks with the global economy: when it works out, all profits are retained by the firms, but when it flops, the government will step in to socialize the losses. So why not take a big chance on financial assets? Indeed, this is the lesson many learned; the management of J.P. Morgan Chase, one of the largest financial firms in the world, actively encouraged risky investment since the financial crisis.[35] And why not? As is commonly said in banking circles, "We have capitalism for when things are good, and socialism for when they fall apart."

The contracts that legally bind most capitalist markets together—facilitated by the state's regulators, police force, and courts—are often not straightforward relations of competitive exchange. They are far more

---

34 This is of course not to say that the capitalist state does in fact "represent" the people.

35 *Guardian*, 3 April 2012; *Financial Times*, 29 June 2012.

complicated, shaped inescapably by nonmarket forces. Markets are social institutions; they reflect the fact that social relations are neither blindly mechanical nor immune to "noneconomic" considerations.

If we accept this, then one way to deal with these information problems might be to base exchange on more intimate social relations. This "communitarian" response is alluring. It echoes a common complaint that capitalism is "greedy" and "antisocial," and that we don't sit out on our front porches anymore. However (leaving aside the nostalgic small-town mythology), in a world where many of the most significant connections we make—political, social, cultural—are widely spatially dispersed, a return to "local community" can help, but it cannot address many pressing concerns. Cities, for instance, are big places, far too big to have a "personal connection" upon which to base all of one's exchange or production relations.

Yet it is true that one of the more effective ways to address principal-agent problems is to build relationships that last over time. A principal might limit information asymmetry by using the same contractor again and again. Even assuming only the most base, self-interested motivations, he or she will have an incentive to treat the principal well: if they don't, and word gets back to the principal, they will not return and future contracts are lost.

LABOUR CONTRACTS

The language of contracts might seem cold and legalistic, the talk of lawyers and bankers. But we all participate in a range of everyday contracts without even thinking about it. The most obvious one is with your employer, if you have one, but there are many others: your relationship to your car or bike mechanic, for example. Many of us trust our mechanics because we have determined over time that they are not going to take advantage of what is for most of us massive information asymmetry. I cannot fix my own car. So, I return to Ed, my mechanic, not because of a utility-maximizing imperative to get the best deal, but because of a relationship of trust that has built up, which often is paired, however irrationally from a cost perspective, with the knowledge that while I may not be getting "the best deal possible," the quality of the relationship makes it make sense. When we act like this (which happens all the time), we are not always acting like "rational," optimizing market participants.

An excellent example of this kind of behaviour is the contractual employment relation at the heart of the capitalist labour market. Employers commonly deal with information asymmetry, and the problems of monitoring workers, by paying higher wages. These so-called "efficiency wages" are intended to reward high-quality workers in order to retain them. They serve two purposes, one at the firm level, the other at the level of the labour market and the economy as a whole. First, firms pay higher wages than would supposedly exist in a "perfect" labour market because even in jobs for which little job-specific skill is needed, there are training costs, and a period of low productivity while the worker is learning. It is also difficult, tiresome, and costly to have a lot of turnover. So firms arguably pay more to keep people after spending all that money and time.

Second, and more important, if workers could make the same money anywhere at any time—which would be the outcome of a "perfect" labour market, since it would result in a single, market-clearing wage for any particular occupation—there would be no income-based reward for staying with a firm. If wages were sufficiently flexible to clear all labour markets, then all firms would pay the same wage for the same work, and all workers could find work (the definition of market clearing). From a worker's perspective, quitting would be virtually costless. From an employer's perspective, commitment to the employee would be useless because they are all replaceable. This would build an unmanageable instability into capitalism, and—as unfortunately little-known economist Michał Kalecki has pointed out—is patently against capital's interests.

As Kalecki puts it, if the labour market ever worked the way neoclassical theory imagines it—if wages were flexible, Say's Law held, and all willing workers found jobs in some orthodox "full employment" dream—then workers would have no fear of "the sack." Without a scarcity of jobs, through which workers get money to participate in the market and put food on the table, capital would lose its power in the labour market. Quit your job? There is another, paying exactly the same, right next door. Thus, while capitalist reason promises that free, unfettered markets will put all the economy's resources to efficient use in an all-engines-firing productive Utopia, in perhaps the most important market of all, the labour market, it has no interest at all in full employment. Full employment would put the workers in charge; indeed, it might even put the unemployed in charge, since they could easily drop in and out of the labour market as they chose, causing trouble in their "leisure" time.

In other words, despite any claims to the contrary, *capitalism must have unemployment*. It is essential to the system's political stability (by disciplining workers) and productivity (by keeping the production process in motion). This only further weakens the edifice of neoclassical "market-clearing" theory, because even if unemployment were not in capital's political economic interest, joblessness would persist. If workers cannot hop from job to job, and employers want a stable workforce, then equilibrium wages determined purely by labour supply and demand are impossible. And if even one flexible price is impossible (remember, wages are the "price" of labour-power), then perfect competition is impossible. This "imperfect competition," a term coined by some of Keynes' disciples, means some firms have more market power, are better to work for than others, and some workers are better at their jobs than others. The competition between the players in this situation, is not just price-based: it will not just lead to a different "equilibrium price." Instead, it will generate price or wage differentiation (or "premia").

Kalecki's point is not only that full employment is impossible in capitalism, but that any substantial effort to provide full employment—perhaps through the state, or reduced work-weeks—would be aggressively opposed by employers. Marx made a similar argument when he said capitalism produces a "reserve army of labour." The reserve army is the mass of unemployed men and women whose desperate need to work looms over those with jobs, and disciplines them into doing as they are told, or being replaced. In Marx's day, however, it seemed that in general, the reserve army was made up of the dispossessed, those driven off the land and out of noncapitalist ways of living, and forced therefore to wait on capitalism's sidelines looking for work. Kalecki's crucial intervention—an elaboration of Marx's insight—was that in contemporary capitalist societies, the reserve army is not external to the capitalist labour process—it is "endogenous," generated by the capitalist system itself.

Virtually all contracts—like many other aspects of markets and firms, and perhaps labour contracts especially—are first and foremost human social relations founded in real space and time, heavily determined by norms, custom, culture, personality, geography, and so on. This has crucial effects both on specific contractual conditions—the prohibition against interest in Islamic banking has driven innovations that allow banks in Islamic nations to still earn profit, for example—and on rather everyday, superficially "noncontractual" realms.

- You apply for a job working for your sister's father-in-law. Do you expect a better chance at the job? Will he hold you to the same standards as others if you underperform?
- You take a well-paying job, but encounter a tyrannical boss. You will never receive comparable wages elsewhere. Do you stay?
- You are hiring for a new management position, and narrow down the list to a man and a woman. The woman is better trained, and thus will cost more to employ, but you know that women are unjustifiably under-represented in management. Who do you hire?

This list is a mild reminder that the market is always a dense network of social relationships, a dynamic emphasized by another prominent theorist of capitalism, Karl Polanyi. Polanyi has been rediscovered by critics of capitalism in recent years for two principal reasons. The first is his argument that capitalism only developed via the evolution of three "fictitious commodities"—things that it must pretend are produced for sale on the market, but are not: land, labour, and money. Polanyi says that none of these are a commodity in the "widget" sense. Yet, because land, labour, and money must circulate on markets like other commodities to make capitalism work, we accept the fiction that they are commodities.

Polanyi's second contribution is his account of modern capitalism's attempt to produce a social structure that "disembeds" the market from its broader historical and geographical context. This allows it to appear "self-regulating," divorced from the life-world in which all human activity is unavoidably embedded. Polanyi argues the market can never be an autonomous realm, independent from social relations in general. There will always be social and spatial relations (culture and geography) that prevent economic activity from achieving anything like a condition of laissez-faire. The upshot is that the contractual relations that define markets and firms in capitalism hinder by their very structure the creation of perfectly efficient, autonomous markets.

Markets in actually existing capitalism cannot be perfectly "efficient," in the sense the term has acquired in neo/classical economic theory. If we ever had markets like that, capitalism would not work. If this is so, it presents a very interesting problem. It means that if the dominant or orthodox theory of capitalism were an accurate description of reality, then capitalism could not exist. This is related to, but still quite different from, the

Marxist idea that capitalism is so internally contradictory that it will eventually implode and become something else. There may be some strategic lessons here. One political conclusion of this analysis might be that to overcome capitalism, we should force it truly to "realize" its theoretical claims—because if it came close to doing so, it would shut down.

I am unsure of this tactic's potential, as it would appear to be quite easily derailed halfway, but it is something anticapitalists should consider. What would it mean for us to embrace "flexible wages" in the interests of "full employment?" Capital says it would love that; what if we gave it to them? It could mean the end of capitalist rule, at least in the workplace and labour market. But this is another instance in which the wage-worker's bind comes into play. Strategies like demanding that capital deliver on promises that would prove its undoing depend on mass solidarity in the face of significant uncertainty. But they give inadequate attention to how we might collectively supply the material security most people need during the struggle, and may need more urgently if it were in fact successful.[36]

Historically, mass movements have arisen due to prior long-term immiseration. But the wage-worker's bind in modern capitalism is effective because, at least in the global North, people feel like they *do* in fact have something to lose. To convince them to lose it—as opposed to merely taking it away—is the principle task of anticapitalist politics, but the constraints are important to recognize.

---

36 See Simon Critchley, *Infinitely Demanding: Ethics of Commitment, Politics of Resistance* (London: Verso, 2007).

PART 2

5

The Long Boom and the Longer Downturn

It is time to put our conceptual material to work on the history of actually existing capitalism. Our focus is the period from the late 1960s to the present, from the collapse of the political economic structures that supported the post–WWII capitalist world to our present age of neoliberal hegemony and financial crisis. Before we get there, however, it is important to briefly consider the relationship between this period and the booming postwar economy of 1945 to the mid-1960s from which it emerged, since the present cannot be understood without some knowledge of the past that produced it.

THE LONG BOOM AND BRETTON WOODS

The quarter-century or so following World War II is often called capitalism's "golden age" or the Long Boom—an era during which the capitalist global North (western and northern Europe, North America, and—confusingly—Australia and New Zealand) experienced unprecedented economic growth, low unemployment, increased average living standards, decreasing income and wealth inequality, and a vast expansion of what we now call the welfare state. The following fifteen years or so, however, roughly 1967–82, saw the whole thing seemingly go to pot. Many thought that capitalism itself was in its death throes. These years inaugurated a process we might call the Long Downturn, a trajectory which, depending upon one's data and interpretation, continues today.

The major (and interrelated) dimensions of this reversal are well-documented, though sometimes controversial. They are usually associated with, among other things, the breakdown of the international political economic regime formally established among capitalist nations at the end of World War II. The agreements that consolidated this regime—known as Bretton Woods, after the New Hampshire resort at which they were signed in 1944—organized postwar international monetary standards, and established the International Monetary Fund (IMF) and the International Bank for Reconstruction and Development (the "World Bank" for short).[37] These "multilateral institutions" continue to wield enormous power in the international sphere, but they were founded for somewhat different purposes than those to which they are currently put.

Bretton Woods (to which Keynes contributed significantly, although the final arrangements differed from his proposals in important ways) had three main formal aims: to promote and fund postwar European reconstruction, in Germany and France especially; to secure

---

37 Bretton Woods also established the General Agreement on Tariffs and Trade (GATT) to monitor and arbitrate international trade disputes. GATT had no binding power, and in the 1990s, it was replaced by the World Trade Organization (WTO), a world free-trade police force, with fully enforceable powers.

the political stability of debtor nations (the UK in particular, whose finances the war had left in tatters, deeply indebted to American finance and the US state); and to stabilize the international monetary regime, which was (correctly) understood to be crucial to the first two goals. Forty-four nations, including the most powerful states in the world and led by the US (which emerged from the war the clear capitalist hegemon), signed the agreements. According to their architects, the institutions would work as follows:

The IMF, using funds contributed by all nations, would provide low-interest loan coverage to debtor states to prevent default during reconstruction and reconversion (the shift from a war-economy to a "peacetime" economy). The World Bank would provide loans or grants for the reconstruction of European (and, eventually, Japanese) economies, a flow of funds greatly enhanced by the US's Marshall Plan, which rebuilt German industry remarkably rapidly in the 1940s and 1950s (the US wanted German demand for its intermediate and consumer goods, so reconstruction was essential). To make all this possible, the international monetary regime was stabilized via a system of "fixed" exchange rates between all major currencies, so all capitalist nation-states had the value of their moneys "pegged" to a specific rate against the US dollar (unsurprisingly, China and the Soviet Union were not signatories). The foundation of the system lay the US dollar's anchor to a gold standard. In other words, its value was pegged to gold, which made the US responsible for the stability of the regime as a whole. Every US dollar was to be backed by—exchangeable for—gold: 1 troy ounce for every 35 US dollars, to be precise.

As discussed in Chapter 3, a "gold standard" is an international currency regime that reigned on and off (mostly on) in Europe and North America from the early nineteenth century to the early 1930s. It is supposed to guarantee the stability of currency values by forcing all participating nations to hold gold reserves equal to the value of all circulating domestic currency. There have occasionally been "bimetallic" standards as well, based on gold and silver, but the principle is the same. The main point of these "convertible" monetary standards is to prevent states from simply creating money when they needed it (to fight wars or fund colonialism) by limiting their money supplies to the value of their reserves, thus restraining inflation.[38]

The gold standard served capitalist purposes for a century or so, but by the early twentieth century, it imposed significant constraints on national and international economies. Most notably, it meant that a nation's economic growth was limited by its gold reserves. If a domestic economy is increasingly productive, then unless the currency increases in value (so that it can purchase more), the new productivity cannot be absorbed by the economy. As a consequence, much of the nineteenth century involved a dog-eat-dog or beggar-thy-neighbour international regime, in which the major capitalist states fought over and hoarded a limited supply of gold, because it was essential to expanding domestic prosperity. (You can imagine why the California gold

---

38 "Convertible" monetary systems get their name from the fact that, at least in principle, all money is at any time "convertible" into its value in the precious metal standard. In theory, this rules out the problem of excessive increases in the money supply (see Chapter 3).

rush of the 1850s was such a big deal for US national development.) In addition, especially at the end of the pre–Bretton Woods, "direct" gold standard era, when every currency was pegged to gold, states were frequently forced to devalue their moneys, i.e., reduce the amount of gold backing each currency unit, to create money to pay for things like World War I (which led most to temporarily abandon convertibility). Most of the capitalist world dropped the gold standard at the beginning of the Depression to fund recovery efforts, and stayed off until Bretton Woods instituted the "indirect" gold standard (indirect because currencies were pegged to the US dollar, which was in turn pegged to gold) that allowed most nations to relax the relentless pursuit of gold.

The Bretton Woods monetary scheme was a system in which all capitalist moneys could in theory move securely in the international realm because their values, and the stability of the economies in which they were based, were guaranteed by an institutional backstop in the form of the IMF, the World Bank, and the general context of American economic power. No need for frantic currency trading, no fears of massive devaluation or overvaluation, and no way for speculators to manipulate or exacerbate exchange rate fluctuations. This is the political economic regime within which the "welfare state" emerged. Capitalist governments across the global North created massive institutional networks aimed at popular "welfare," and paid for them with so-called Keynesian deficit financing.[39] The expanding social function of the

---

39 Although the term "Keynesian" has come to describe the deficit-financed welfare function of the state, as discussed in Chapter 2, it is in some ways quite far from what Keynes' theory suggests and the policies he endorsed. While he recognized the

state was certainly not entirely attributable to the Bretton Woods framework, but its stabilizing of state and super-state institutions was part of what helped the welfare state make sense.

Although it is unfortunately beyond our ken to follow up the Long Boom in detail, from a growth, social security, income equality, and wage-rate perspective, it was more successful than any previous international or national mode of economic organization—capitalist or noncapitalist. Of course, not everyone enjoyed the fruits of this "success." It entailed—indeed, it depended upon—a vastly unequal distribution of political economic power and the further geographical concentration of wealth in the global North. Still, from the perspective of accumulation pure-and-simple, little in human history can compare. Its successes were all the more exceptional when set against the backdrop of the most recent "peacetime" economy in the memory of many: the Great Depression. It is crucial to keep this relative achievement in mind when confronted with liberal and "progressive" nostalgia for the postwar welfare state. In Europe and North America, unions in particular seem stuck in a rueful political paralysis imposed by the weight of the postwar experience in the lives of an older generation of workers.

THE BUSTED BOOM AND ITS ORIGINS

The Long Downturn is closely associated with the collapse of the Bretton Woods regime, since many of the dynamics it was designed to suppress or eliminate in the

---

temporary need for state debts, he was no fan of permanent welfare mechanisms. Indeed, the massive infrastructure of the modern welfare state would have almost certainly alarmed him.

mid-1940s raised their ugly heads two decades later. By the late 1960s, the fixed-exchange-rate regime was falling apart. Food and commodity prices rose, driving inflation and inviting speculation. Oil prices skyrocketed (rising 400 percent), and the advanced capitalist world experienced a severe decline in productivity growth (the increase in output per unit of labour). This slower rate of growth ignited distributional conflict between labour and capital, and between different fractions of capital. This fanned the inflationary flames higher, as different social groups and classes fought to retain their piece of the income pie, exacerbating political instability.

How all this came about is the subject of some of the most heated historiographical battles in recent memory, and not only among historians. How the story gets told suggests who is to blame, what we can do about current troubles, and whether or not the "golden age" is in fact recoverable. Many on both the left and the right argue that the sources of the Long Boom's exhaustion lay not in some new, unanticipated dynamics, but in the era's very "successes," that its achievements sowed the seeds of its own decline. The following points are standard evidence for this argument:

- Low unemployment levels empowered labour, which demanded a bigger income share (which exceeded 66 percent of total income in the US by the late 1950s, compared to 58 percent in 2011), and had the wherewithal to back up those demands, thus reducing profit and slowing innovation.[40]

40 Margaret Jacobson and Filippo Occhino, "Labor's Declin-

- High capacity utilization (the proportion of productive resources actually in use) and growth increased demand and stressed supply, causing inflation.

- Europe and Japan benefited from the post-war reconstruction efforts, importing advanced American technology and production systems. They "caught up" with the US, challenging the Bretton Woods political economic hierarchy, which was explicitly structured with the US at the top.

- Existing technologies were pushed to their limits, reducing the Long Boom's unprecedented rates of productivity growth.

- The isolation of planned economies (i.e., state socialisms) allowed them to grow also—not without problems, of course, but enough to offer an alternative path to developing countries, thus fanning domestic opposition in the capitalist core.

One of more notable features of this explanation is its rather "orthodox" flavor. Anticapitalists often reject it for that very reason, especially, it seems, because it more or less blames the end of the Boom on workers. In fact, much of modern economics is premised on the ill workers do when they get too much power. Orthodox theories of inflation, for example, cloak themselves in "monetarist" supply theories, but almost always blame

---

ing Share of Income and Rising Inequality," Federal Reserve Bank of Cleveland Economic Commentary, 25 September 2012, http://www.clevelandfed.org/research/commentary/2012/2012-13.cfm

inflation in the real world on labour's excessive demands. They may call for monetary restraint, but the main "political" reason they do so is to limit wage demands. Capitalist common sense says that excessive money supply increases the price level via "wage-push" inflation.

This underlines the fact that how we explain the crisis of the 1960s and 1970s is not merely "academic." On the contrary, it is enormously important today, both politically and economically, because we are constantly struggling over what lessons the past teaches. Different interpretations of the past lead to different conclusions regarding what can be done at present. But we must not reject orthodox explanations just because they are orthodox. In fact, capitalist reason provides some very helpful tools for understanding capitalism. There are aspects of contemporary economic life that appear to be very well diagnosed by conventional tools. Rather than rejecting orthodoxy because of its ideological predisposition to posit capital as the engine of historical progress, even in periods before capitalism itself existed, and to see workers and noncapitalists as "backward" forces, hindering progress, we need to see it for what it is: a set of ways of understanding the world that is a product of the very world it is trying to explain. Capitalist reason is embedded in and emerges from a particular, ideologically saturated world. Recognizing the embeddedness of "reason" in its time is about as close to truth as we are ever going to get with respect to actually existing human communities. We have to resist the desire to dismiss it out of hand, and search instead for the truth in it, truth of which that reason might not itself be aware.

The historiographical battle over the end of the Long Boom is a useful example of this. Labour activism and workers' growing expectations *did* play a significant role in pushing capitalist political economies to the point of collapse. The employed and unemployed *did* demand more, women and non-European or nonwhite workers *did* enter the labour force in enormous numbers and expected (but rarely received) reasonable compensation, and unions and other civil rights organizations did obtain, however temporarily, some power to trouble capital's hegemony and its rate of wealth accumulation. One need not be a right-wing monetary economist to expect capitalism to be in trouble in such a situation. The point is not who is to blame—a question of interest only to those wanting to "save" postwar capitalism—but rather what happened, why, and what lessons can be learned.

Surely one of the main lessons is that demands from workers and others outside the halls of power can, over time, really do a number on the system. Of course, an organization like the United Auto Workers, for example, which certainly played a part in these struggles, was and is by no means anticapitalist. It has never been interested in upsetting capitalism or its key institutions. If the UAW had its way, the Long Boom would have been Longer, ideally Eternal. But that does not mean we cannot learn from the UAW's experience.

Let's try to put some meat on these polemical bones by returning to history itself. It is worth remembering that rapid postwar growth and urbanization across the global North led to a massive decline in agricultural employment, both absolutely and as a percentage of the labour force, and a corresponding increase in industrial and service employment. What drove these changes was the rapid accumulation of capital over the period (i.e., "growth"). Increased capital stock—objects of capitalist investment like factories and technology—usually brings with it employment growth.[41] This process was concentrated in urban regions, so the growth was urban-biased and led to an increasingly urban population and economy across the board.

Low unemployment and urban concentration was a boon for labour organizations that, in turn, demanded and obtained regulatory adjustments like higher unemployment benefits, reductions in hours, and job protection legislation. This further increased the power and size of organized labour. The extent of these effects varied (less extensive in the US, quite a bit more extensive in Scandinavia, for example), but in almost all cases organized labour became more bold, and the level of industrial conflict grew. (Wage statistics show that strikes and conflict worked: wages and benefits increased. This pattern no longer holds.)

These rapid and substantial wage increases (especially compared to earlier periods in capitalism), had two important, if predictable, effects. First, they squeezed capitalist profits. This problem was intensified by accelerated inter-capitalist competition between US firms and those Japanese and German businesses benefiting from postwar reindustrialization, which prevented capitalists from raising prices to pass increased labour costs on to consumers. Second, it helped generate inflation, by increasing the costs of production and expanding demand for existing consumer goods (better-paid workers buy more things, and are willing to pay more for them).

In other words—and I don't think it is possible to exaggerate the importance of this for understanding the

---

41 Whether our present slump is an "exception" to this rule, or a new rule altogether, remains to be seen.

development of the neoliberal, financialized capitalism we live with today—the crisis that ended the good ol' days of the Long Boom was a *distributional* struggle. Orthodoxy almost never says this explicitly, but it is right there in its account of the history of capitalism. This struggle had two fronts: (1) a struggle between labour and capital over the distribution of income—an increasingly empowered labour-force wanted more of it; (2) a struggle between nationally based capitalists over the distribution and control of productive power and international market share. One might also add: (3) conflict between highly developed rich countries and resource-rich but less powerful countries. Keeping the latter in mind would help us rethink the standard explanation of some important political economic developments. For example, the massive OPEC oil price increases of the early 1970s, which most Europeans and North Americans are taught was merely random and baseless Arab nastiness, makes much more sense through this lens.

States played a key role in these developments, mostly by attempting to manage or contain the distributional conflict. On the first front (domestic class struggle), states faced the choice of either inflating or deflating their way out. They could either (a) let money supplies and government spending increase so workers really did feel like their wages were going up, and businesses felt like their profits were maintained; or they could (b) clamp down on inflation by reducing government spending, raising interest rates, suppressing wages and benefits, and tightening up the supply of money and credit in circulation.

At least at first (in the US under Nixon and Ford, for example), capitalist states generally chose to inflate their way out of the crisis, hopefully subduing distributional conflict by keeping profits *and* wages high while maintaining investment and consumer demand. If both groups wanted a bigger piece of the pie, and dividing it was a zero sum game, then the state figured it would just increase the size of the money-pie and try to keep everyone happy. The choice to inflate—which merely postponed the crisis—is not at all surprising. By the early 1960s, most capitalist states were already on a path of growing government employment and spending, a response both to popular pressures (for pensions, protections, health care, etc.), and to increased state revenues, which made previously unaffordable social services possible. Moreover, although things have obviously changed, it used to be that states providing effective social services could expect public support, so it was smart politics too. This is the welfare state as we remember it.

As for the struggle between different national capitals, most states' main goal by the late 1960s and early 1970s was to survive the exchange-rate chaos created by the breakdown of Bretton Woods. The breakdown was largely attributable to the decay of macroeconomic conditions in the US: its attempts to manage its own domestic distributional struggle in the manner just described, to pay for Vietnam, and to cover for a loss of international competitiveness, which led to surging imports and falling exports. The American response to this situation had an enormous impact on the whole capitalist world because of its role as the linchpin of the Bretton Woods system. Since all currencies in the system were fixed to the value of the US dollar at a specified rate (with the interesting exception, for much of the time, of the Canadian dollar), and the US dollar was in turn valued at a fixed amount of gold, when the US devalued its currency, it not only reduced the amount of gold the dollar was worth—which let it increase the money supply—it also exported inflation around the world.

This sounds more complicated than it is. Under Bretton Woods, the value of every other internationally significant currency was measured relative to the US dollar. So, when the US devalued the dollar, it unilaterally devalued every other Bretton Woods currency. This not only passed the costs of Vietnam and US domestic turmoil on to the rest of the world, it put the whole international system of economic management at risk. By 1971, there was no way the US could devalue any further and pretend to be the bedrock of the international monetary system, and it dropped the gold standard completely, initiating on its own terms the "floating" exchange rate system we have today. These developments challenged the hegemony of the US dollar and American power, and, for a time, severely limited the capacity of firms in the most influential capitalist states to assert their dominance over firms and states outside the global core. The situation was made worse by the oil crisis of 1973–74, which exacerbated inflation and the profit squeeze, and reduced real wages (since it substantially increased most workers' cost of living). The result was reduced investment and consumer demand.

So the Long Downturn that followed the long boom *was* at least partly a product of that boom's successes, just as most orthodox accounts suggest—if for different reasons (they usually blame it all on state spending and uppity workers). The eventual response to the crisis, in the

1970s and early 1980s, took a little while to configure. But when it came, at least in North America, the UK, and parts of western Europe (Scandinavia was an interesting exception), it brought the reassertion of capitalist discipline. It put capital back on top of the political economic hierarchy—it had never really been usurped, but it had been forced to cater to the rabble—by choosing domestic conflict management option (b) above: clamp down by reducing government spending, raising interest rates, suppressing wages and benefits, and tightening up the supply of money and credit in circulation. This hurt capital in the short term, and support among business people for this radical economic restructuring was by no means unanimous, but in the long term it was one of the most brilliant moves it ever made. This turn to inflation control marks the consolidation of the neoliberal capitalist state in the industrialized world.

The principal objective was to reverse course on the distributional conflict strategy: to give up on the conciliatory attempt to inflate our way out of crisis, and force markets to swallow a bitter pill and deflate. In other words, the state, with the particularly vocal support of bankers, decided to kill inflation, no matter what the social cost. If you remember (Chapter 3), modern monetary policy is oriented toward inflation control using so-called interest-rate operating procedures (increase interest rates, subdue inflation; lower interest rates, allow a little price increase). This obsession with inflation has stood as macroeconomic common sense since the beginning of the downturn we are discussing. (It is, however, presently being questioned by a whole host of players, from Joseph Stiglitz to the IMF he attacked so vigorously after his time at the World Bank, although this change of heart seems to be a matter more of expedience than repentance.)[42]

What we know today as "neoliberal" policy was established at this time, and not just in monetary policy, but across the whole realm of capitalist economic management. It was the moment when business, and finance capital in particular, started to reassert control of an economic system that had throughout the post–WWII era been increasingly influenced, if never dominated, by labour. In doing so, it not only retook the political economic reins, but got in a few retaliatory kicks as "payback" to working people.

COUNTER-REVOLUTION AND EMERGING NEOLIBERALISM

Following the analysis of political economist Andrew Glyn, we can describe the components of this strategy as "austerity, privatization, and deregulation" (although "reregulation" would be better; more on this below). Glyn says these involved a "counter-revolution" in macroeconomic policy (fiscal austerity, restrictive monetary policy), the retreat of government from many arenas of economic life via deregulation and privatization, and the "freeing" of labour market dynamics, in particular by repealing or not enforcing worker protections and union-friendly legislation.[43]

This counter-revolution, and in particular the attack on inflation, was no straightforward boon for capital. It could not be; when economic activity tanks because of

---

42 Joseph Stiglitz, *Globalization and Its Discontents* (New York: W. W. Norton, 2003); Jonathan Ostry, et al., "Capital Inflows: The Role of Controls," IMF Staff Position 1004 (2010).

43 Andrew Glyn, *Capitalism Unleashed* (Oxford: Oxford University Press, 2006).

high interest rates and low demand, most businesses are not happy. Moreover, capital is not some homogeneous monolith; there are different, often conflicting, fractions of capital and competing international and domestic capitals. What is good for one fraction or region is not necessarily good for all. Inflation is a case in point. In its mild variety, it helps some businesses, especially those indebted to banks and other financiers or relying on exports—in the first case, because the dollars with which the loan is repaid are cheaper; in the second, because inflation reduces the value of your currency relative to other moneys, so your goods become cheaper for foreign buyers. But by the mid-'70s, inflation had reached a level that could not be called "mild," and it was making unemployment worse. It is fair to say that pretty much nobody was happy.

This situation—high or rising inflation and unemployment, so-called "stagflation"—seemed to contradict the fundamental tenets of "Keynesian" economic theory. Capitalist governments across the global North, Scandinavian left-social democrats and US right-conservatives alike, faced a difficult dilemma. This was especially true with regard to growing unemployment, to which even conservatives are sensitive given its influence on election outcomes. If states chose to try to stimulate spending with loose money and fiscal programs, inflation would almost certainly accelerate. If they chose to clamp down on state spending, drive up interest rates, and choke off inflation, the effects on unemployment were sure to be terrible. In the end, as I mentioned, many of the most powerful nations struggled from the late '60s to the late '70s, arriving at option two after experimenting with option one.

One of the more common paths this transition took—in Canada, the US, and the UK among others—had three basic steps:

1. As the crisis took hold, the government, with the approval of both capital and labour, tried to inflate and/or stimulate the way out of it. By the early 1970s, increasing inflation proved this tactic ineffective on its own.

2. By around 1972 or 1973, the government attempted a "planned" alternative: continue to stimulate while suppressing inflation by *fiat*, i.e., they made inflation against the rules, via wage and price controls like those used during World War II. These "incomes and prices policies" involved union commitments to reduce wage demands and employer commitments to keep prices from rising at such rapid rates. This did not work, and pleased no one.

3. In the mid- to late 1970s, the state gave up trying to please both sides, abandoned labour and small business, and embraced finance-friendly Chicago-style economic policy: jacking interest rates and slashing government spending.

The best-known example of step 3 is the so-called "Volcker coup" of 1979–82. Paul Volcker was appointed chairman of the Federal Reserve (or the "Fed," the US central bank) at the end of Jimmy Carter's single presidential term, and remained through most of Reagan's term of office.[44] The Volcker coup is best described as the use of US monetary authority to squash inflation no matter how many jobs, how many social services, or how much human welfare it cost. In a period of only a few months, Volcker pushed US short-term rates up from about 5 percent to about 15 percent (and that was just the federal funds rate—the rate at which banks borrow reserves from each other—retail rates, the ones you and I have access to, were far higher). The rapid rise in rates slowed the economy to a crawl, and borrowing, investing, and spending dropped off a cliff. Inflation fell from 13 percent in 1980 to 3 percent three years later.[45]

The objective, as I said, was to choke off inflationary pressure, to protect the domestic value of the US dollar, whose purchasing power was diluted by inflation. In turn, this would buoy its value on foreign exchange markets, which had fallen significantly in rapid inflation, reducing American economic power, and making the US dollar a much less useful tool of geopolitical influence. With the dollar plummeting, for example, why would OPEC countries want to keep it as the currency used to buy oil? Dollar devaluation reduced oil revenues. So it was important to kill inflation and save the dollar for both domestic and internationally strategic reasons.

---

44 Alan Greenspan, whom is commonly blamed (only partly justifiably) for the subprime crisis, succeeded him in 1987, and directed the Fed until 2006.

45 As an aside, Volcker has been in the news again recently, in his role as special economic advisor to President Obama. He has been especially visible with regard to new banking regulations he proposed and presented to the US Congress, which would limit banks' ability to play the gambling game with their clients' money—regulations, interestingly, he would likely have opposed when he was Fed chair.

But why did the dollar's value relative to other currencies fall in the first place? It fell because when a country experiences inflation, the purchasing power of its currency declines, and basically becomes a losing bet: you buy it on the international currency exchanges today, when it can buy x, y and z, but when you sell it tomorrow, it can only buy x and y. In a mode of production in which value is the form wealth takes, it does not make sense to hold your wealth in a money that is diminishing in value. Consequently, when inflation is a problem for a country, other countries and financial institutions don't want to hold their currency, so they try to sell it. When they offer it for sale, they find almost everyone else is trying to sell it too, creating an oversupply on the market, which only further reduces the value.

In recent history, the US dollar has been less subject to these vicissitudes than almost every other currency because of its centrality to the world economy. Even since it gave up its place at the hub of the Bretton Woods system, it remains the currency with which nations buy oil, and the form in which many, if not most, countries hold their foreign reserves (the liquid assets the state sets aside, almost like a savings account, to cover international expenses, purchase foreign exchange for imports, etc.). However, this starring role causes a lot of trouble when the US dollar loses value, or threatens to lose value. A declining US dollar affects many other nations; certainly every advanced capitalist economy, and no small proportion of developing countries as well. Some of them are hurt even worse than the US. As noted earlier, Nixon's attempt to inflate his way out of crisis was not only directed at domestic problems. He was also effectively trying to export inflation, and reduce the real value of the US foreign debt (since the dollars in which the US owed its debts would be worth less than those originally borrowed).

These dynamics highlight an essential driver of the financialized global economy, a driver that is sometimes obscured by everyday "common sense." Common sense tells us, for good reasons, to think of interest rates as a *cost*. Most of us, after all, are consumers in some way or another, and many of us are debtors too: credit cards, payday loans, car or student loans, mortgages. So when we see "Interest Rates Rising" in the headlines, we think, "Oh, that's bad." For us, it means the things we need or want to purchase, especially big-ticket items like houses and cars and educations, will cost more.

But a significant part of the global economy—arguably the most important part—is coordinated by people who understand things in a completely different way. If you are a lender, or a bond trader on international money markets, when you see "Interest Rates Rising" on the front pages, you think, "Excellent." For you, interest rates are not a cost, but a return that makes you money. If interest rates rise in a nation, that makes its currency more, not less, attractive to many international players. Not only can that country's currency buy more on international markets, but its bonds offer a higher return. So in many cases, the interests of finance are diametrically opposed to those of (some) businesses and almost all household consumers. What you and I experience as cost is their return. And, for good or ill, the international economy (especially the money and capital markets), operate according to their preferences, not ours. Whenever we are talking about global capital, there is a significant portion for whom interest rates are profit, not cost.

There are exceptions, but for finance capital, it is fair to say higher is better (to a point, of course; you don't want capitalism to collapse because no one can get credit in a major economy—this was partly what Keynes feared).

To return to our story, a rising dollar and US high interest rates in the wake of the Volcker coup had substantial but unequal effects on different groups in the US. Not only did high interest rates make borrowing very expensive, which basically stopped manufacturing growth dead, but export-oriented manufacturers were put in a tough spot by high currency values, since it made their goods more expensive for foreign purchasers.

A BRIEF BUT CRUCIAL ASIDE ON BOND MARKETS

This trade impact is one manifestation of a crucial problem in international capitalist political economy, one very important from a social justice perspective. When an economically influential nation like the US changes its interest rates, especially when it makes its currency and bonds more attractive to finance capital and foreign investors, it affects virtually every other nation in the world. Like the US, at any one moment in time, most nations owe money to international creditors, or want to raise money, say, to pay for domestic infrastructure. The principal arena of this international credit and debt activity is the notorious, much-discussed-but-rarely-explained "bond markets."

Because bond markets are so important to modern capitalist governance, it is worth pausing to explain how they work. Here's how: if the government of a nation—Brazil, for instance—wants to pay for infrastructure, service some debt, or undertake other major expenditures, the principal means to obtain the necessary funds is the international bond market. To raise the money, Brazil must issue bonds, which are also called "debt," in the form of repayment contracts of predetermined length. Bonds have a face value, known as "par" (say $100,000 for this example, but they can have smaller denominations), and a predetermined "maturity" or term, at the end of which they are "redeemed." Most states issue both "government bonds" (denominated in their own currency) and "sovereign bonds" (denominated in a foreign currency, usually a widely trusted "reserve" currency, like the US dollar), for a wide range of maturities, from one month to thirty years. In other words, states sell bits and pieces of their debt (i.e., the claim to a certain amount of repayment from that state), which purchasers then hold, and for which they are repaid once the debt contract is up. Most states, especially in the developing world, tend to auction five- and ten-year-term debt, but in this brief explanation we will use one-year bonds, since the idea is the same and we don't have to work out compound interest.

In this example, each bond represents a claim on the Brazilian government for $100,000 in one year's time. Since bond dealers are not going to purchase bonds for "par," to be repaid the same amount they loaned with no interest on top, most bonds with maturities of more than a year have a "coupon rate." The coupon is the annual interest rate the issuer promises bond-holders, who will also get the "par" value when the bond is redeemed at maturity. In addition, when the Brazilian state auctions or "floats" bonds (usually with the help of, and often heavily backed by, an investment bank like Goldman Sachs or JP Morgan), not only must it offer a guaranteed annual return in the form of the coupon, but, because it is an auction, the issuer cannot command a particular price for the bond. If you are the US, whose bonds are in high demand (especially when considered a "safe haven" in crises), you might be able to sell your debt at a "premium," i.e., for more than par. But if you are Brazil, you will most likely have to sell your debt at a "discount," less than par. Participants in bond markets—big financial institutions and some foreign states—examine sovereign credit history and rating (Brazil is a BBB, a rating determined by the same credit agencies that did such a good job leading up to the subprime crisis) and a host of other factors, and then decide whether or not to bid, and if so, at what price. Once sold, purchasers can either keep bonds until maturity and redeem them, or sell them to another bond trader in the meantime. Whoever is holding them will receive the coupon payments (usually semi-annual), and will bring them back to the Brazilian state to redeem at maturity, to receive the face value.

The tricky, if unsurprising, part is that for Brazil, bond traders will demand a sizeable incentive as an encouragement to lend (i.e., buy bonds). They worry about Brazil's capacity to redeem them in a year, or that its currency will tank and either devalue the bond or force the state to issue new bonds with a higher coupon, or that social unrest or a collapse of the governing coalition might bring a new government that tells global finance capital to shove their bonds where the sun don't shine. So traders focus not only on the coupon, but on what is known as the bond's "yield," or the profit they can anticipate if they were to hold the bond to maturity (a function of both the coupon and its sale price).[46] The higher the coupon, and the greater the discount, the larger the yield. The larger the yield demanded by bond traders, especially relative to other nations' bond issues, the larger the risk "the market" deems the purchaser to be taking. From a percentage perspective, the difference is the same as an interest rate, if an "implicit" one.

Let's follow through on the Brazil example to see what this means in practice. For the purposes of convenience, and because we are using a one-year bond as an example, we will assume a "zero-coupon" bond, meaning that all the investment risk is calculated into the difference between par value ($100,000) and the discount Brazil must offer to attract investors. As I write (Spring 2012), Brazil's $100,000 bond issue with a zero percent coupon and one-year term will fetch less than $89,000.

---

46 If the bond were purchased at par, then yield will be equal to the coupon rate, and if the bond were purchased at a premium, yield will be less than the coupon rate. But if the bond was purchased at a discount, then yield will be greater than the coupon rate. In other words, if Brazil sells a $100,000 dollar bond for $89,000 dollars, then when the bond is redeemed, the purchaser profits not only from the coupon payments, but also from the $11,000 deal on the original purchase (because they bought a bond for $89,000 that they redeem for $100,000).

The coupon rate and the difference between par and the bond's sale price indicate how large a return investors must be promised to give them incentive to purchase the bonds. This is also affected by a country's inflation rate, which is almost never zero (in Brazil or elsewhere), and can be quite a bit higher in Brazil. This is one reason Brazilian government bond yields are so high. Inflation eats into bond dealers' profits by reducing the real value of the money in which the bonds are redeemed. This is part of the explanation for finance capital's and modern capitalist states' shared obsession with controlling inflation.

In comparison, if Canada auctioned a $100,000 bond with a one-year term and no coupon, bids might come in at about $98,500.

To see how this works like an interest rate, let's use these same numbers: Brazil auctions its $100,000 bond for $11,000 less than face value, Canada can sell its for $1,500 less. From a bond trader's perspective, it looks like this: "If this investment works out, we will earn $11,000 profit from a $89,000 one-year investment in Brazilian bonds, and $1,500 profit from a $98,500 one-year investment in Canadian bonds." Which is to day that the potential annual return from investing in Brazilian bonds is $11,000 ÷ $89,000, or approximately 12.4 percent. The return on Canadian bonds is $1,500 ÷ $98,500, or about 1.5 percent. These percentages ("yields") are just like an interest rate charged on a loan by a bank; the bond purchaser is like the bank, and the bond issuer the borrower.[47]

Bond yields are extraordinarily influential in modern capitalism. If a country must offer higher yields to sell its debt, all else being equal, it is costing them more to borrow money. They are for all intents and purposes "subprime" nation-states. As the not-at-all fanciful Brazil/Canada comparison shows, this can make a big difference, and at the volume of money that can change hands at a sovereign bond auction it is enormous. Brazil might well sell $500,000,000 debt in a year, but a half-billion-dollar, one-year bond issue will raise $54,500,000 less than a Ca-

---

47 A more complex variation on this process is exactly how interest rates are set in the capitalist states of the global North: via what would, in any other situation, be considered market manipulation, the state buys and sells its own bonds in an effort to control interest rates.

nadian bond issue of the same amount and duration. If that were not burdensome enough, bond yields also have a massive impact on domestic interest rates. Domestic banks will lend to local enterprises only at rates competitive with what they can earn by investing their money elsewhere. If they are confident they can get 12 percent return on their money buying bonds, they are going to need a lot of convincing to lend to a local firm for less.

The same dynamic operates at the international level. If a wealthy nation widely trusted by international finance (i.e., "credit-worthy") were to offer high yields, then yields offered by a nation like Brazil will look less attractive. With no fear of revolutions or regime changes, every big player in the bond market is going flock to the wealthy nation's auction unless others can match the yield, if not beat it by an attractive margin. So, if the US, for example, is offering great rates to global financiers, then no one is going to buy Brazilian or any other bonds unless they offer even higher returns, since they are not considered as credit-worthy as the US. Moreover, most vulnerable developing world countries are excessively indebted to the IMF, the US, and others, debts that are frequently short-term and denominated in US dollars (which rising interest rates make more expensive and which exports thus have less power to earn). Short-term debt, combined with domestic structural problems that cannot be solved in the short term, means a developing nation cannot meet its obligations to international lenders and bond-holders. It is thus forced to renegotiate the terms of the outstanding debts at different (punitive) interest rates.

In the context of the current financial crisis, the US is not offering high yields on its bonds. On the contrary, they are lower than at perhaps any previous moment in history. As I write, the US can almost borrow money on the international capital markets for free. The yield on a one-year Treasury security, for example, is 0.19 percent. If inflation is higher than that, the US state enjoys a negative real interest rate—international financial capital is effectively saying it is willing to pay for the right to lend to it. But back during the crisis that led to the Volcker coup (to return to our story), US interest rates skyrocketed, and other nations had to follow suit, just to prevent international finance from dropping their currencies and bonds in favor of those of the US—and in the process killing non-US exchange rates and economies. So, with the Volcker coup, the rest of the world had to raise their rates to comparable levels, meaning the Fed's vicious recessionary monetary policy rapidly diffused across the globe.

One of the better-known results of this process was the Latin American debt crisis. In the early 1980s, many Latin American countries (and others too) who had borrowed enthusiastically throughout the 1970s were forced to renegotiate the terms of international loans. They found themselves in a market demanding exorbitant interest rates, up to 20 percent (compared to 6 or 7 percent in the mid-1970s).[48] They could never agree to these loans and expect to actually meet their payment

---

48 These are nominal interest rates. The change in real rates (nominal rates minus inflation) was even greater, and perhaps more meaningful: in 1975, real international interest rates sat at -2.9 percent. In 1981, they hit 8.1 percent, an increase of 11 percent. Sources: Economic Commission for Latin America and the Caribbean, *Economic Survey of Latin America and the Caribbean* (Santiago: ECLAC, various years); IMF, *International Financial Statistics* (Washington DC: IMF, 1987), 113.

obligations, and many defaulted. The whole continent went into a decade-long tailspin.

FROM LIBERALISM TO NEOLIBERALISM

What I have discussed thus far in this chapter is a set of processes frequently grouped together under the umbrella concept "neoliberalism." Neoliberalism is a term currently used only by its critics; its champions, including the leaders of most capitalist countries, do not proclaim themselves "neoliberals." If you hear the word today it is almost certainly used derisively. Indeed, for a while, "neoliberalism" was used everywhere in radical or progressive circles to describe the ills of the modern political economic order. However, although there are some good reasons for describing that order as "neoliberal," only occasionally did anyone bother to say what neoliberalism was, or why it named anything more than a remarkably successful form of capitalism.

At first, I was unconvinced of the need for the term, but I was so relentlessly dressed down for my skepticism by people I respect that I eventually decided to take it more seriously. I am glad I did—because I was wrong. Neoliberalism may indeed be remarkably successful capitalism(s), but it is not adequately understood on these grounds alone. My error was first exposed when I looked at how "neoliberalism" helped explain the work of the IMF.

The IMF is one of the most important frontline units in the diffusion of neoliberalism beyond the wealthy world. It has been a key player in many of neoliberalism's most notable disasters, including the institutionally imposed starvation, poverty, and indebtedness due to the global North's so-called "management" of the Latin American debt crisis. Much of this devastation is associated with the IMF's role in the "structural adjustment" of developing world national economies. Although the IMF was not originally designed to do this work, by the 1980s one of its principal objectives was to remove what it identified as "structural" obstacles preventing client states' "integration" into the global economy, especially via trade, but also via financial flows. The means to this end are now known as "poverty-reduction strategies" (formerly "structural adjustment plans")—contractual conditions the IMF imposes on its borrowers, including changes in governance borrowers *must* undertake to receive an IMF loan. Until the Eurozone crisis (see Chapter 7), these borrowers were mostly developing countries.

Why, in the IMF's view, is international economic integration good for everyone? The IMF's policy programs are designed with particular theories in mind. On the economic side, we have the classical political economy discussed in Chapter 2—the ideas of Adam Smith and the neoclassical economists and policy makers who consider themselves his modern disciples. The political theory side is underwritten by a doctrine that goes hand in hand with classical political economy: classical liberalism.

"Classical liberalism" gets its name because (a) it is "classical" in that it came before the modern age; and (b) it is "liberal" because it believes, for reasons that Smith and others laid out, that society should not be "constrained" by the state or any other force, because the individual freedom to seek out opportunities for profit and utility is the necessary corollary of the idea that the pursuit of self-interest is the golden road to collective wealth. The IMF may not describe itself as "Smithian" or "Ricardian," but its approach adheres pretty closely to Smith's and Ricardo's views (at least as they are understood by modern neoclassical economists). And their views, as you will remember, suggest that anything that prevents specialization, trade, and innovation—anything that prevents enterprise from pursuing profit—is a bad idea.

So, to return to my initial resistance to the term "*neo*liberalism," how different is the new variety from classical liberalism? Clearly, it uses new technical tools and institutions (like credit default swaps and the World Trade Organization), and it dominates economic knowledge production across the globe in a way the original liberalism never did. But is it really any different from what was going on in the UK and the US in the 1920s? Or Britain in the 1850s, for that matter? To answer this question, let's return to the IMF. Its constituent policy prescriptions have three main objectives, which, in the case of the IMF's loans, become "conditions" that must be met to receive funds:

1. Liberalization (drop tariffs, subsidies, capital controls, export restrictions, etc.)
2. Privatization (sell state holdings, which in many cases are substantial)
3. Stabilization (allow currency to float at its "natural" [usually lower] exchange rate)

As this outline of the neoliberal policy package shows, neoliberalism is not merely a way to specify the modern variety of classical orthodoxy, but a description of at least two powerful and intertwined contemporary economic dynamics: *globalization* and *financialization*. Neoliberalism can be understood as the historical conjuncture, and political legitimization (via both coercion and consent) of these two processes. Globalization is the integration of the international economy via trade. The original version of liberalism certainly involved globalization, but without the kind of financialization we have today with *neo*liberalism—or at least, back then, finance played a different and subordinate role as investor in productive enterprise.

However simplified, this definition of neoliberalism is helpful since it allows us to identify some of its novel historical and geographic dynamics. It enables us to understand the differences between what is sometimes called the "first era of globalization"—British free trade imperialism in the nineteenth century—and what we call globalization today (by which we mean something more specifically neoliberal). In the first era of globalization, the era of classical liberalism, the term meant international economic integration via trade and production networks, especially trade in goods and primary commodities. Indeed, as measured by international trade, the first era of globalization was as integrated as the present.[49]

In our present era of neoliberal globalization, the term means international economic integration via

---

49 Increased international trade does not necessarily mean "liberalized trade" in the contemporary sense. While the first era of globalization saw a massive increase in international trade (in exports as a proportion of economic activity, for example), this does not mean that trade was "free" and went wherever it chose. This was the height of British colonialism and, in reality, very few countries and colonies participated in, or benefited from, the explosion in global trade.

trade *and* financial channels. In contrast to the first era of globalization, today the movement of goods and services, and the flows of often untethered capital, are equal but often independent partners. Obviously, they are not always working together for the same purposes, nor do they always cooperate (think about the possible differences of opinion between finance and industry on interest or exchange rates mentioned in Chapter 3). My point is that "neoliberal" globalization is driven as much by finance as by trade, whereas nineteenth-century "liberal" globalization was dominated to an extraordinary extent by traders. The former was the logical form a capitalist internationalism that emerged in a mercantilist geographical and political matrix would take. It also explains free trade imperialism's dependence on colonialism, the geographical infrastructure mercantilism produced. Wall Street's "relative autonomy" from "Main Street" today would have been impossible in the nineteenth century, when finance was the handmaiden of a Main Street economy that enriched itself via mercantilist methods.

The simultaneous explosions of financialization and globalization in the last thirty or so years have been interdependent. There are times when they help each other and times when they hinder each other, but they both depend on similar policy environments. It is difficult these days to integrate internationally via trade and escape the reach of global finance. Technological change has also played a big part. Much of global trade would be impossible without recent improvements in transportation, refrigeration, etc. And, technology has also been a key factor in the capacity of finance to shape globalization, especially increases in the speed and volume of information transfer across space and among market participants. In addition, the technical and analytical changes made possible by computerization (especially complex modeling and "financial innovation") have facilitated the "securitization" of income flows virtually anywhere on the globe, at almost any point in the future.[50] This has surely helped financialization to accelerate, and even take the lead in, neoliberal globalization.[51]

What David Harvey calls "space-time compression" may be the best way to understand the neoliberal era, and how it differs from the classical era. He uses the concept to describe how the dynamics of capitalist development effectively blur the distinction between space and time (at least from an "economic" perspective), while at the same time they work to shrink or compress this new space-time. The idea was first developed in depth by Marx, in his notebooks now published as the *Grundrisse*. The gist is that capitalism tends to evolve in a way that makes problems posed by space (lengths of supply chains, geographical barriers like oceans, the physical structure of urban space)

---

50 Securitization is the process through which rights to regular flows of future income—from consumers' credit card payments, students' loan payments, homeowners' mortgage payments, pensioners' life insurance payments, and more—are decomposed and reconstructed so as to be transferable on financial markets (see Chapter 6 for detailed explanation).

51 There is an important chicken-or-egg problem here. To what extent is technical change in any particular instance a cause or an effect of economic change? Many technical advances are initially developed for military applications, but that does not make the question any easier to answer, since the role of militarism in modern capitalism (driver? effect? both?) is not clear either.

increasingly indistinguishable from problems posed by time (the time it takes to realize return on investment, or the slowdown in economic activity at night). Over time, technological change has meant that spatial problems that used to seem insuperable are increasingly understood in terms of their temporal features. It is easier to get commodities to and from major centres on the other side of the world than it is to nearer but more remote locations. As long as communication and transportation are cost-effective and reliable, there is no spatial limit to the length of a supply chain or other contractual relation. Similarly, spatial strategies can overcome formerly insuperable time constraints. If financial markets have to shut in New York because people have to sleep, then an integrated set of global financial centres, in which it always daytime somewhere, can eliminate traditional dead time when no money could be made. Everything gets sooner and closer. One could see nineteenth-century "liberal" globalization in this light, but it was more accurately an attempt to deal as profitably as possible with given "natural" obstacles to capital accumulation.

Indeed, a defining quality of that earlier, liberal globalization—both states and enterprises—was long-term commitment to economic projects. Insofar as profit was based mostly on commodity production and trade, and on the quite slow (by modern standards) movement of goods, long-term commitment was absolutely necessary, both in political (colonization) and economic (commodity extraction and manufacture) dimensions. In the accelerated time-space compression of neoliberalism, long-term commitment has not vanished; it lives on in the expansion and increasing complexity of supply chains, for example. However, the volume and pace of economic flows have risen exponentially due to finance, which has taken special advantage of the profitability possible in the increasingly short "instant," the unit of neoliberal time.

Defining Neoliberalism

Given the above, let's suggest a definition. Neoliberalism is the ongoing effort, in an inevitably uneven global political economy, to construct a regulatory regime in which the market is the principal means of governance and the movement of capital and goods is determined as much as possible by firms' short-term returns. Because that global political economy is dynamic, neoliberalism is always incomplete, and is itself uneven.[52]

Neoliberalism—as a policy program, political project, or historical variation of capitalism—can never be "finished." As soon as anyone thinks all the loose ends have been tied up, the very dynamism of capitalism (and the social world as a whole) changes the terrain and more neoliberalization work has to be done. The vigilance this situation requires makes neoliberalism far more flexible and agile than is often assumed. Its policies and regulations necessitate a nimbleness that is well-suited to a regulatory regime in which the movement of capital and goods is determined as much possible by almost instantaneous changes in short-term profitability. This remarkable regulatory regime can make it possible to earn or lose hundreds of millions of dollars in the few

---

52 The neoconservative pundit Thomas Friedman may have made millions telling us otherwise in *The World is Flat: A Brief History of the Twenty-First Century* (New York: Farrar, Straus and Giroux, 2005), but the world is definitely not flat.

minutes following an earthquake in Honduras or a brief shift in exchange rates.

This is a crucial aspect of neoliberal political economy that we find echoed in the rise of finance (see Chapter 6). Neoliberalism is not just about getting rid of rules, or "deregulation." Removing tariffs, capital controls, currency pegs, restrictions on foreign ownership, and so forth are all essential elements of neoliberal regulatory programs, abolishing rules that limit firms' opportunity to maximize short-term returns. But states and firms and international institutions need not only to eliminate rules, they must also create new ones, imposing, extending, or deepening regulatory or legal structures where they were previously underdeveloped or nonexistent. For example, countries the world over have established intellectual property rights regimes for everything from medicinal plants to corporate logos, often where no such legal frameworks existed before. That is not deregulation by any stretch of the imagination. Jamie Peck and Adam Tickell were among the first to point out these complexities in "actually existing neoliberalism," which they label "roll-back" (deregulation) and "roll-out" (reregulation). Neoliberalism has always involved both.

As for the use of the market as a means of governance, one of the best examples can be found in the IMF's standard structural adjustment policy package. By force-feeding nation-states its neoliberal medicine, the IMF produces a situation in which the market—foreign exchange markets, global commodity markets, and/or equity (stock) and bond markets—becomes the principal means though which the behaviour of nation-states, firms, and individuals is governed. When the package is accepted (however forcibly) by a borrower-state, it is effectively accepting that markets have the ultimate power over its behaviour—judge, jury, and executioner. Insofar as market-mandated conduct is precisely the goal of neoliberal policy regimes, who better to govern it than the market itself? "Bonds not bombs," we might say—if it were ever that simple.

6

From the Rise of Finance to the Subprime Crisis

The term "Long Downturn" would seem to suggest a broad and general dip in the fortunes of the states and economies of the capitalist global North. But if we look in a little more detail, we find that it describes a shift affecting different places and sectors unequally. Indeed, more than perhaps any other sector, it was manufacturing that took the hit, and experienced the most significant downturn at the end of the Long Boom and the onset of the crisis of the welfare state, a tendency that diffused across the economy because manufacturing was arguably the most important sector from an employment perspective.

The forces behind this shift are the subject of much controversy. There is no agreement on what mattered the most, or where its origins lie. Most residents of the wealthy nations will be familiar with the story of the collapse of "good" manufacturing jobs in much of Europe and North America, and the rise of "sweatshops" in the global South, who for subsistence wages now do what "we" once did for "good money." At a macro scale, it must be said, this story is pretty much true, although its political reasoning can serve reactionary and progressive causes equally well—many efforts to defend this or that nation's working class unfold quite nicely along exclusionary and nationalist lines. Nevertheless, it is essential to remember that however important it was or is, manufacturing never comprised the entire North American or European economy, neither forty years ago nor today. If every sector of the rich world's economies had experienced the problems that have plagued their manufacturing sectors since the early 1970s, their capitalisms would be in much worse shape than at present.

FINANCIALIZATION

A more dramatic collapse was avoided because—as every teenage job-seeker (at least in North America) is told over and over again, in an effort to prepare them for the rigours of the "real world"—while manufacturing declined in its relative contribution to economic activity, something called "services" expanded correspondingly. The category "services" covers an enormous range: from coffee shops to hair salons, consulting firms to internet service providers, from auto repair to health care, and more. It also includes "FIRE": finance, insurance, and real estate. FIRE contains a whole host of activity; financial services on its own includes retail and investment banking, investment advice, accounting, stock brokers, tax services, etc.

The growth of services' relative contribution to economic activity has been enormous (as measured by conventional indicators like gross domestic product, or GDP). Still, despite what many of us might imagine when we think of services, growth in incomes from the service sector is not primarily a function of the number of coffee shops and sushi restaurants, but of other services—and to a substantial degree to the "F" in FIRE. Financial services' contribution to overall economic activity has skyrocketed since the late 1970s, from almost nothing to 8 percent of GDP in the US.[53] That might not seem like much, but we must remember it means

---

53 Measuring aggregate economic activity is a complicated process, and the quantitative indicators economists and policy-makers use are fraught with categorical, technical, practical, and ethical problems. GDP is a classic case. Even if we set aside—as almost everyone almost always does—the problems associated with measuring or valuing "capital" that Keynesians have been demonstrating for decades, GDP still causes economists trouble. Among other limitations, it can only measure what gets recorded as spending and thus both misses a significant amount of economic activity and depends upon firms' and individuals' reporting; it attempts to measure only "domestic" economic activity in an era in which the line between "domestic" spending (inside the nation-state) and "national" spending (by any government, firm, or individual based in the nation-state) is only arbitrary; and it has no way of managing the qualitative differences in what money is spent on, so that what you pay for medical care after a bicycling accident contributes just as positively to GDP as spending on your or your child's education. In addition, GDP has no sensitivity to distribution; if in a nation-state with 100 citizens, one had an income of $1,100, and all the rest had incomes of $1, then if the rich citizen's income doubled and everyone else's stayed the same, the national economy would appear to be doing twice as well, while in actual fact the relative (and most likely absolute) poverty of 99 percent of the population declined. These measurement issues multiply, because GDP is the basis of many other key policy indicators, like inflation. There are ongoing efforts on the part of "heterodox" economists to replace GDP with a better measure of overall economic activity and well-being, but alternatives have yet to be widely taken up. I use GDP here only because it is the form in which data are presently available.

that almost one dollar in ten that moves in the US is associated with finance. Moreover, compared to other large diversified economies, 8 percent is quite large, and much larger than it used to be, especially during the capitalist "golden age" of the post–World War II boom. Eight percent is not that different from the sectoral ratios of nations commonly associated with much greater dependence on finance, nations that have established themselves as regulation- and oversight-free capitalist oases. These nations, many of them "offshore financial centres"—or, more colloquially, "tax havens"—like the Cayman Islands or the Bahamas, have hitched their economic wagons to global finance capital, attracting wealth and income flows with the promise of little regulation, no tax, and secrecy. Singapore, which many think of as a massive city-state organized around international capital flows, has only a little more of its GDP based in finance than the US (the UK is also comparable to the US; Canada is notably less finance-centric).

The story is even more interesting if we focus on corporate profits as opposed to overall spending. That 8 percent is American finance's contribution to all domestic expenditure, a total that includes spending unassociated with, and not oriented toward, profits: state expenditure (government programs, health care, education, etc.). Relative to the proportion of the economy that is profit-seeking, finance's contribution is much greater, and growing. It now accounts for more than 40 percent of all corporate profits in the US. Even with economic conditions as bad as were following the financial crisis that began in 2007, 40 percent of all corporate profits is an astounding amount of money, and it has a corresponding influence on the economy and its governance.

Moreover, these figures still understate the matter, since they describe domestic profits alone, earned inside or repatriated to the US. They take no account international subsidiaries. Yet much of the world's financial industry is based in London, Shanghai, etc., where all major North American firms have offices, wholly owned subsidiaries, and extremely active trading desks.

The increased role of finance in overall economic activity and the increased proportion of profits that are realized via financial channels are the two main empirical indicators of a process called *financialization*. I would like to suggest we work with both a general and a more technical definition of the term. First, in general, financialization describes the increasing role of financial motives, financial markets, financial actors, and financial institutions in the operation of domestic and international economies. Second, from a more technical or specific perspective, financialization is a pattern of capitalist accumulation that relies increasingly on profit-making through financial channels, even for capitalists that are not themselves financial firms.

How and why has capitalism become increasingly financialized over the past three or four decades? What does this mean for capitalism, present and future? There is a great deal of debate among political economists over financialization, and even more over where it's headed. The answers I offer here are partly my own, and partly drawn from accounts I find compelling.[54]

---

54 These include Giovanni Arrighi, *Adam Smith in Beijing* (London: Verso, 2010); Robin Blackburn, "The Subprime Crisis," *New Left Review*, series II, no. 50 (2008), 63–105; Robert Brenner, *The Economics of Global Turbulence* (London: Verso, 2006); Andrew Glyn, *Capitalism Unleashed* (Oxford: Oxford

To understand the rise of the financial sector—and its associated rise in political power—and to understand the processes of accelerating financialization more generally, we must begin again with the end of the Long Boom, focusing on a series of more finance-specific developments made possible by the macroeconomic changes described in Chapter 5. As with other aspects of the Long Downturn, only an understanding of dynamics behind the 1970s crisis of capitalism can make sense of what has happened since in the realm of finance capital. We must reject the popular idea that the rise of finance (or any other economic change of the 1970s) is an unprecedented restructuring or innovation in economic dynamics, unrelated to what came before. Instead, we can only explain the drastic changes brought about by financialization—a central component of the phenomena associated with neoliberalism—if we put it in the context of the post–World War II economy in the developed world.

At the most rudimentary "economic" level, the rise of finance can be traced to the general fall in the rate of profit in the post–World War II era. The decline began

University Press, 2006); William Greider, *Secrets of the Temple: How the Federal Reserve Runs the Country* (New York: Simon and Schuster, 1987); David Harvey, *A Brief History of Neoliberalism* (Oxford: Oxford University Press, 2005); Geoffrey Ingham, *The Nature of Money* (Cambridge: Polity, 2004); John Lanchester, *I.O.U.: Why Everyone Owes and No One Can Pay* (New York: Simon & Schuster, 2010); Stephen Marglin and Juliet Schor (eds.), *The Golden Age of Capitalism: Reinterpreting the Postwar Experience* (Oxford: Clarendon Press, 1990); Lance Taylor, *Reconstructing Macroeconomics* (Cambridge: Harvard University Press, 2004). They range from the fairly technical (Taylor) to the reads-like-a-good-thriller (Greider) to the hilarious (Lanchester). All are excellent.

almost unnoticed, when on the surface all seemed to be well. Even in the "golden age" discussed at the beginning of Chapter 5, the rate of profit was actually declining in the US. But "business sentiment" remained high until the late 1960s, as did the rate of investment, which suppressed the effect of falling profits.

Investment stayed up for a variety of reasons, two of which are arguably most important. First, the political peace between big labour unions, big business, and big government (part of what gets called "Fordism") that characterized this era provided, in a broad sense, a guarantee of high wages, low industrial conflict, and high profits. This reassured capitalists that they would make good money on their investments, even if the overall rate of profit seemed to be dipping a little. Second, rates of capacity utilization, consumption, and government spending meant that even if the profit rate or share was in slight decline, aggregate profits (in terms of amounts of money) stayed strong, which was further reason to invest.

But in the late 1960s, the rather slow fall in the profit rate accelerated markedly, and continued steadily until the Volcker coup of 1979–82. If you have to pick a birthday for neoliberalism, this is it. It had been gestating for a number of years, but more than any other single event, the Fed's interest rate shock (helpfully coupled with Reagan's assault on social services and unions) reasserted the dominance of capital in US political economic relations, and by extension throughout much of the developed North. It did so by restarting the profitability of very large corporations, the financial sector in particular. Remember how much they hate inflation?

During the 1970s, rates of investment jumped all over the place: up in response to intermittent monetary and fiscal stimulus by the Nixon, Ford, and Carter governments, and down when inflation retook centre stage. Then, with Volcker's interest rate hikes, which made investment too expensive for many businesses, everything slowed to a crawl. In combination with the political economic forces that caused problems for the welfare state (like increasing international competition and giving more power and voice to workers), these trends led firms to look for ways of making profits other than through Long Boom–style brick-and-mortar investment.

This makes perfect sense. A firm that sees fewer and fewer opportunities for profit—in the work it does, the markets it serves, or the regions it produces in or sells to—will look around for other opportunities. This is exactly what the 1970s general decline in the rate of profit led US firms to do. And it led to a search for financialized profit. When US investment banks post record profits in the middle of the worst capitalist recession since the 1930s, as they did in 2010 and 2011, the overwhelming success of that search is evident. So while it is certainly true that for manufacturing in particular the Long Downturn has lasted since the 1970s, and that this has had important employment and productivity effects, it is essential to remember that the entire economy did not suffer the same fate as the manufacturing sector after the late 1970s. In fact, by the early 1980s, profits even began picking up generally, as many firms, both financial and nonfinancial, turned to financial channels to produce or protect returns.[55]

---

55 The post–World War II rate of profit in the US reached its peak right in the mid- to late-1940s, immediately after the war ended. Although there have been some drastic downs and some exuberant ups in the intervening years (the early 1960s and the

In other words, instead of building plants to augment production, or searching for new markets, many firms took existing profits and invested them in financial instruments, of which—due to computational novelty ennobled by the term "financial innovation"— there was increasing variety to suit an investor's particular needs. New financial securities either spread investment risk across sectors, times, places, and political-economic risk profiles, or they concentrated them in one sector, or focused on a specific set of flows or eventualities. They could even be customized—an innovation especially important to the insurance industry—whereby firm-specific contracts established a flow of funds over time that could then be marketed to other investors or used as collateral to raise funds to finance further investment.

This reorientation, and the relative smoothness with which financial innovation made it possible, is one of the most important developments in the history of global capitalism. How firms did this—how they renovated themselves for making money via financial channels—reveals much about neoliberal regulatory transformations. Although people barely talk about it any more, not so long ago most capitalist nation-states had regulations that severely constrained firms' ability to be financialized in the manner they are today. Many of these regulations are known by the umbrella term "capital controls," and they matter enormously to this story because, when North American capital started looking

---

late 1990s, for example), the overall pattern is steady decline since then. Neither the renewal of profits in the mid-1980s, nor the financialized booms of the late 1990s and early 2000s led to rates of profit comparable to those of the "golden age."

for ways to generate profits via financial means, they discovered many opportunities abroad. They found foreign stock markets and other financial instruments, or foreign currencies to protect themselves from the falling value of the US dollar. They could purchase bonds from growing economies like Germany.

But during the Long Boom, many governments constructed elaborate regulatory structures to limit or prevent capital movements into and out of a country. The US had the most capital to invest in other places, but the US government was convinced that it would be best to keep as much investment as possible inside the country. This was another lesson drawn from proper "Keynesian" policy. Why let domestically-generated investment capital help other countries grow, when it can create jobs, stimulate technical change and economic growth, and provide tax revenues at home?

The US engineered a whole suite of capital controls, covering many different activities (other countries did the same, but the US rules were the most important for global capitalism). Two of the best known were the "interest equalization tax" and "Regulation Q." The first imposed an export tariff on all US capital leaving the nation at a rate that equalized opportunities for financial profit at home and abroad. In other words, the US government said: "Sure, go ahead and invest in foreign assets, but the tax you pay to do so will make it not worth doing."

Regulation Q capped interest rates on domestic demand deposits (basically savings and checking accounts, the bank services from which it is relatively easy to "demand" your money, in contrast, say, to a mutual fund). This was designed to (a) discourage local banks from depositing their money with big banks, and instead to lend local locally, and (b) limit competition among banks, thereby ensuring the stability and survival of those same local banks. Unsurprisingly, Regulation Q's limits on financial profit sent wealthy people and institutions in search of other places to put their money, especially money markets and markets for other financial instruments. This only increased the pressure driving the financialized profit-seeking that the interest equalization tax (among other legislative means) was supposed to contain.

In a context of declining domestic profit rates, these regulations led firms with the organizational capacity to establish offshore financial arms, mostly wholly owned but independent subsidiaries. This period (1964–73) marks the rise of largely unregulated "Eurodollar" markets—markets in US dollars and financial assets that operate outside the US and beyond its jurisdiction—eventually centred in London. Offshore capital flight continued throughout the late 1960s, 1970s, and early 1980s. Eurodollar markets exploded, abetted in particular by the diligent cultivation of the UK's Thatcher government, elected in 1979. The plan was to remake the UK as a centre of global finance capital, thereby re-establishing Britain's international political economic standing, which had waned considerably since World War II. Thatcher's government was explicitly interested in enabling "the City" (London's equivalent of Wall Street, which had thrown its considerable financial and organizational resources behind her election campaign) to steal some of New York's high-powered thunder.

To make this happen, the UK government's main effort, and its main achievement, was the radical deregulation of finance in the UK. The success of these efforts, which unsurprisingly attracted money-capital from all over the world, drove the deregulation of all main financial channels around the industrialized world. "Financial innovation" blossomed as national authorities across the capitalist global North and beyond were forced to scrap the regulatory apparatus slowly constructed since the Depression to compete for the flow of investment funds. Money markets—which the influential economist Joseph Schumpeter called "the headquarters of the capitalist system" as far back as 1911—exploded in size and sophistication. Increasingly sophisticated technologies of securitization—the seminal steps toward the financial instruments, like "collateralized debt obligations," that have received so much recent media attention—disseminated rapidly across international asset markets.

Ultimately, these developments produced a significant shift in the centre of gravity of international economic activity. Institutional lending has exploded, but the years since the late 1960s have witnessed an almost constant increase in the ratio of firms' borrowed funds (borrowed from financial institutions) to gross capital formation, a trajectory only checked by the problems that began in 2007. In other words, firms are borrowing more, but putting a smaller and smaller share of it toward capital formation (plants, training, research and development, etc.). Leverage—financespeak for borrowing money to invest, in the hope that return on investment will more than repay the loan—expanded to an extent unimaginable even thirty years ago. Indeed, up to the financial crisis triggered by the collapse of the "subprime" mortgage market in 2007, astoundingly precarious leverage ratios had become the normal way of doing business in finance. Before the investment bank Lehman

Brothers collapsed in September 2008, it was levered 44 to 1. That is to say, it had outstanding loans valued at 44 times the value of its assets. If called upon to repay, which of course it eventually was, it could have covered a little bit less than 2.3 percent of its debt.

However useful spectacular failures like Lehman Brothers are in emphasizing the imbalance and cumulative myopia of modern capitalism's systemic imperatives, it is perhaps even more important to note that financialization is not confined to the financial sector. Since the 1990s, both financial *and* nonfinancial firms have eagerly participated in this dynamic. Nonfinancial firms—even firms that do regular old things like manufacturing—now try as often as possible to make profits via financial channels. And they do not do so merely via their own enormously profitable "financial" arms, like car manufacturers endlessly offering "the lowest APR" to help finance the purchase of their products. We are talking about a process whereby, at least up until 2008, nonfinancial firms increasingly invested their income in financial instruments like corporate bonds, mortgage-backed securities, futures, and the like (see below).[56]

However novel all this seems, "new" developments like financialization are often mistaken for radical breaks with the past when they are in fact the outcome of previous conditions. When the Nixon administration of the

---

56 The person who has done most to help us understand the dynamics of this process across the modern capitalist economy is the sociologist Greta Krippner. See especially her ground-breaking 2005 article, "The Financialization of the American Economy" (*Socio-Economic Review* volume 3, no. 2, 173–208), and *Capitalizing on Crisis* (Cambridge: Harvard University Press, 2011).

late 1960s and early 1970s chose to loosen money (inflate) rather than drive down costs (deflate)—a dilemma that would have been familiar to governments of the early 1930s—it was a fateful decision. The limits of the inflationary "postponement" option for the protection of profits became increasingly apparent as the 1970s unfolded. The pace of capital flight to international money markets accelerated, productivity growth slowed further, and domestic investment and employment fell again and again. The "financialized" way firms escaped falling profits established the foundations for the current neoliberal regime.

Of particular importance for future neoliberal governance, these dynamics reignited capital's zeal for stable money, an obsession the Keynesian interlude had tried to suppress. The financialized solution of the 1970s and after meant a growing proportion of capital, and a huge proportion of its overall profits, depended more than ever on the suppression of inflation. The profitability of financialization is a straightforward function of monetary stability. Profit accumulated via investment in a financial instrument is diminished by every rise in the price level: if you earn 10 percent profit on an investment, but inflation is at 10 percent, then in real terms your profit is zero.

Moreover, although significant monetary instability will always curtail investment (if the value of money is plummeting, investment seems unwise), a price level rising at the lowest possible rate, or not at all, actually hinders nonfinancial capital formation: mild inflation (in the 3 to 8 percent range, say) is almost always a part of expanding effective demand, and the profits reaped from investment in nonfinancial productivity make a little inflation less troubling. Financial investors, on the other hand, don't really give a damn about overall economic activity or productivity, except indirectly, i.e., if it slows the accumulation of wealth via financial channels. And what is good for finance is by no means always what is good for the rest of us. In North America, the two decades in which finance became king of the profit world were years of constant declining productivity and workers' real wages.

By the late 1970s, as capital searched frantically for ways to make financial profit because the old ways didn't seem to be working, the absolute and unquestionable necessity of capitalist control of monetary authority became glaringly obvious. Volcker's shock is the best-known instance of this power grab, but the Reagan, Thatcher, and Mulroney administrations of the 1980s, and every American, British, and Canadian government since, have recognized and acted on this imperative. They did so because they all understood that suppressing inflation was predicated on silencing workers, not only to support employers suffering from "wage-push" profit squeeze, but also, and perhaps even more importantly, to protect financial capital and financial profits in economies that were in many ways no longer productively competitive. Finance was about the only realm in which these governments made good on their promises to turn declining incomes around.

Financialization since the 1980s is a product of these longer-term dynamics, as are the fundamental political challenges it creates. The increasing power of monetary authority over its fiscal sisters and brothers, initially stamped so powerfully upon the planet by the Volcker-era Fed, has become normalized. As many have noticed, and as the early responses to the current crisis demonstrated, fiscal policy—taxes, public spending on services and infrastructure—has been effectively and intentionally crippled (and its recent, crisis-inspired new lease on life seems very precarious). Monetary authority is king of the macroeconomic mountain, and the extraordinary accumulation of power in the hands of the Fed and the European Central Bank (ECB) are definitive proof. This is a victory not only for finance and financialized capitalism, but for classical and neoclassical orthodoxy, neither of which could have won the day without the other.

The task of challenging the structures that protect this elaborate privilege is made all the more difficult by the fact that monetary policy-makers in capitalist liberal democracies, as discussed in Chapter 3, are no longer accountable to elected representatives or their constituents. Central banks now control the key arena of monetary authority, and, given the wide belief among neoclassical economists and neoliberal policy-makers that democracy has an inherent "inflationary bias" (that is really the phrase), the consensus "best practice" among all leading capitalist nations is to put these institutions "in the hands of unelected technocrats with long terms of office and insulation from the hurly-burly of politics" (in the words of a noted Ivy League economist and central banker).[57]

---

57 Alan Blinder, *Central Banking in Theory and Practice* (Cambridge: M.I.T. Press, 1998), 58. The need to de-democratize monetary governance is not merely some extreme market fundamentalist article of faith. Blinder is not a Chicago School free-marketeer who accepts monetary absolutism as a regrettable but necessary feature of modern capitalism. On the contrary, he has recently been one of the more "reasonable" liberal critics of financial deregulation.

This is no accident. The dominance of monetary policy is absolutely essential to modern capitalism. Indeed (as discussed in Chapter 5), it has allowed the neo-liberal state, interlaced as it is with finance capital, to appear to have separated the market from the state, while nevertheless *using* the market to govern the behaviour of workers and firms. In this sense, financialization has two aspects: it is a strategic priority for capitalist firms and a political priority for the state, which itself becomes dependent, both for tax revenues and overall economic stability, on this marketized mode of social organization. In terms of the relative value of income flows, these processes affect firms much more than households. From a money-making perspective, the financialization of the capitalist global North is more about businesses than consumers. Nonetheless, households, and not only those of the rich, have taken part in very important ways, largely through the skyrocketing accumulation of debt.

The forces behind increased household indebtedness are several. First, the general stagnation of wages since the 1980s. When your nominal wages do not rise at the same rate as the cost of living, or perhaps even fall, then the real value of your income declines over time. To keep consuming at the same level, you must borrow and eat up your savings (if you have any) to cover the loss of real income. Clearly, millions of households ended up in this situation. Household savings rates collapsed, across North America especially, as many owed more than they could possibly bring in. Second, with the overall expansion in available credit, especially after the mid-1980s when interest rates came back down and most financial regulations had been rolled back, a lot more money went into circulation via the bank channels discussed in Chapter 2. All that money, and relatively slower change in what was available to buy—especially in property markets—meant that more money was chasing the same amount of stuff. The result was inflation, which meant real wages fell further. In addition, businesses helped accelerate the problem because they needed to spend more to get the same real level of investment. Both consumers and business borrowed to make up the shortfall.

The result was the rapid financialization of much of everyday consumption via "securitization." More and more of everyday life became marketable, by finance, to other institutions. Securitization is the process through which rights to present and future flows of income—consumers' credit card payments, students' loan payments, homeowners' mortgage payments, pensioners' life insurance payments, and more—are reconstructed as material assets that can be exchanged on financial markets. The combination of this excessive financialization of the economy and increasing firm and household indebtedness turned out, unsurprisingly, to be a toxic mix. Even Wall Street analysts now admit that the very forces that drive financialization create the seeds of its implosion. This is not exactly news: Marx, Keynes, and others had been making the point for close to two centuries. Today this argument is most closely associated with the late economist Hyman Minsky, who went from being a little-known hero of "post–Keynesians" to a household name in 2008. Minsky says the structure of capitalist finance always leads to increasing risk-taking; in "good times," capital tends to creep farther and farther out on the leverage limb, an endeavour that by definition cannot go on forever.

When the bough breaks, it produces crises like the one we have right now.[58]

SUBPRIME: A CASE STUDY IN NEOLIBERAL FINANCIALIZED CAPITALISM

Let's make things a little more concrete by going over the recent "subprime" crisis in some detail, in light of the dynamics discussed in the previous chapters, as an instance—both typical and atypical—of capitalist dynamics in general and contemporary, neoliberal capitalism specifically. Considering the crisis from different perspectives will help us understand both the details and broader political economic issues. This involves a three-step investigation, starting at the systemic level, moving "down" into the details of subprime mortgages and securities themselves, and then back "up" to the institutional level. We will conclude by positioning these processes in the principal structures and relations of contemporary capitalism.

I lay this out in four subsections: (1) lays out the overall processes that led to the possibility of a credit "bubble"—financialization, the East Asian crisis, the dotcom bust, and low inflation + low interest rates; (2) looks at the way all that easy credit made its way into the hands of borrowers, i.e., how subprime mortgages work; (3) explains in broad brush-strokes the securitization process by which these contracts entered the financial

---

58 The implosion of the subprime mortgage market in the US is frequently called a "Minsky moment." Minsky's argument can at times get a little "technical," but it is really worth a read. See "The Financial Instability Hypothesis—A Restatement," in *Can "It" Happen Again?* (Armonk, NY: M. E. Sharpe, 1982), 90–116 (the "It" in the title is the Great Depression).

circulatory system; and (4) considers how what we know about capitalism can help us understand all this.

(1) The Systemic Causes of the Liquidity or Credit Bubble

The "subprime" moment did more than anything else to trigger the 2007 crisis, but its specifics are embedded in, and meaningful because of, the decades-long, system-wide processes of financialization and associated capital flows discussed above. The collapse of the subprime market may have unlatched the gates of the financial crisis that enveloped much of the world, but it did not "cause" it.

Nevertheless, it is helpful to set this structural context aside momentarily and start with some key features of global political economy that allowed the crisis to take the subprime form it did. This is a story in which China, perhaps surprisingly, plays a lead role. China is crucial to the health of global capital. Its massive and tumultuous growth depends entirely upon demand for its manufactured exports, and however capitalist or noncapitalist China's domestic economy is, the concentration of demand in Europe and North America means China has hitched its wagon to the capitalist world. As wages, productivity, and nonfinancial innovation in the capitalist world have declined, so should the international purchasing power of US and European consumers. Given what economists call the underlying "fundamentals" of the US economy, setting aside its role in the international realm, the US dollar should have declined significantly in value over the last three or so decades. The US exports fewer goods, borrows more and more relative to its productive capacity, and the income of much of its population has fallen significantly.

Yet, given Chinese industry's orientation toward US markets and offshore manufacturing for US (and European) firms, a precipitous fall in US consumption must be avoided at all costs. Consequently, the Chinese state has taken upon itself, especially since the mid-1990s, the task of continually propping up the value of the US dollar and the level of US spending by purchasing US government debt. The Chinese commitment ensures sufficient demand for American debt, which keeps US bond yields far lower than if they were assessed according to the standards by which other nations' debts are judged. Consequently, the US has been able to borrow enough from China (and other Asian nations) to keep its interest rates low and its consumption levels high. Since much of that consumption demand targets Chinese goods, the cycle continues.

Where does the Chinese state get the money to keep purchasing US debt? Well, for a variety of reasons and despite very low wages for the vast majority of its labour-force, Chinese savings rates are very high. This is probably a function of both cultural norms (which are certainly not fixed, but tend to change relatively gradually) and the low wages and export-orientation of Chinese industry. High saving propensities and low incomes mean that until very recently, China's domestic consumer markets were relatively underdeveloped. These conditions produced a glut of savings in China. Much of it, at the firm level, is in US dollars (because they sell to Americans). These savings purchase US debt, making China the largest holder of that debt (Japan is second).

This political economic strategy has drawbacks that render it potentially unstable. While it ideally has the capacity to prop up international consumer spending, China's own pretensions to geopolitical leadership are hindered by playing a supporting role in global political economy. If Chinese capitalists and the Chinese state want to assume a leadership role, China must divest itself, at least to some degree, of its dependence on the US in particular. But this would entail putting its own economic engine at risk.

This situation is further complicated by other dynamics in Asia, many of which are linked to the Asian financial crisis of 1997–98. Among the more devastating of its legacies was the massive devaluation of Asian currencies, largely a product of speculative investment and "hot" capital flows, which fled the region when the crisis began with the collapse of the Thai currency (the baht). Speculative or hot money is an important aspect of neoliberal political economy, a product of precisely those forces Keynes and others hoped to abolish with Bretton Woods, forces that have been unleashed anew by the dismantling of that regime.

If you are unfamiliar with the dynamics of the Asian financial crisis, here are the basics boiled down: in the midst of the boom that powered the growth "miracle" among the "Asian tigers" in the late 1980s and 1990s, the Thai currency came under speculative attack by currency traders working for powerful US and European financial firms. Such speculative attacks follow a standard pattern. Traders first begin to hammer on the currency of a relatively vulnerable nation-state like Thailand by "shorting" it, thereby driving down the value of the currency on international money markets.

Shorting is a fascinating and powerful trick of the financier's trade. Since the whole point of shorting is to make money as an asset *loses* value, it is somewhat counter-intuitive for many nonfinance folks, but essential to understand. To "short" a financial asset, a stock, a commodity future, or anything else is to bet that its value is going to drop. In anticipation of this change in price, the shorter borrows some of that asset (say, 10,000 shares or $500,000 in currency) from someone betting the other way. They contract a date at which the borrower must return the same amount of the asset to the lender (plus some fee for the loan). Since they think the asset's price is going down, the "shorter" sells the assets immediately. If they are correct and the price does indeed fall, then, when the loan comes due, they buy back the same assets for cheaper, return them to the lender, and keep the difference.

The most important things to remember about shorting are (a) as long as there are at least some others out there willing to bet against them, traders can make money when asset prices are going up *or* down; and (b) if there is a speculative frenzy, when everyone expects something to drop in price, the prophecy is self-fulfilling: as everyone shorts the asset, they flood the markets with "for-sales," which forces the price down and makes traders' expectations come true.[59] Indeed, if the traders are big enough players, they don't have to rely on the

---

59 There are even common ways of getting around the fact that when prices are obviously tanking, it is hard to find someone stupid enough bet the other way and lend assets to the would-be shorter. This so-called "naked" shorting is risky, but prior to the crisis it was a widespread practice, and continues in many jurisdictions.

markets to help them produce panicked selling; they can influence the market enough to create the panic themselves. Whether driven by the interests of one firm or by the oligopoly that controls the currency trade, this is a particularly nasty example of the exercise of market power. For a national currency like the Thai baht, it is a disaster.[60] But not for the traders, of course, who bought all the currency back when it hit bottom, waited until international bailouts and time raised the value again, and then sold it anew. They made money all the way down, and all the way back up.

Speculative currency shorting (usually) targets a weaker nation in the global political economy, because stronger nations can fight back by using reserves to purchase their currency on those same markets, thereby maintaining demand and protecting the currency's exchange rate. It would be impossible (and potentially suicidal, I suppose, at least at present), for bond markets to mount a speculative attack on the US dollar. Thailand had little capacity to defend the baht, and its value plummeted. The ensuing panic engendered similar attacks on other "Asian tiger" currencies, and the frantic flight of hot capital from the whole region. This only drove currency values down further, because as money leaves a country, unless it is the US dollar, it almost always changes form—the money-owner exchanges it into US dollars or some other "trustworthy" currency.

---

60 Because shorting can wreak havoc, and because largely deregulated financial asset markets and complex "innovations" in securities have made shorting an everyday practice, it played a key part in the 2007 financial crisis. One of the first (and only) meaningful regulations the US imposed in the months immediately following the collapse of the market in subprime mortgage-backed assets was to ban some forms of shorting.

This floods the market with (for example) baht, which accordingly falls in price.

The tiger economies' inability to protect their currencies is widely attributed to a lack of state-held foreign reserves. They learned, consequently, to maintain a huge pile of reserves, in case history repeated itself. They also decided it is smart to keep a lot of those reserves in the form of US securities, because this gives them some capacity to correct exchange rates on their own, even if the US decides not to help much. If the US dollar over-appreciates, thus diminishing the rate of return on sales to the US (because a higher value dollar can buy more exports), then selling some US debt can help depreciate the dollar a bit. Only China and Japan really have the capacity to unilaterally move the market like this. China and much of coastal Asia spent the late 1990s and early 2000s flooding the US with money, accumulating reserves in the form of US bonds, and in the process, giving the US government and consumers billions and billions of dollars to spend—ideally on Chinese and southeast Asian goods.

One notable result of this process was the so-called internet or dotcom bubble, fueled by indebtedness built on Asian (and especially Chinese) debt purchase. When, at the turn of the millennium, the ecstasy of dotcom became the agony of dotcon, not only did the Fed set very low interest rates to stimulate recovery, but a steady supply of money of Asian origin made the "easy money" policy even easier.

For a variety of related reasons, simultaneous with these developments, American banks were completing a business model transition that accelerated foreign capital inflows. Banks' traditional way of doing business, sometimes called the "net margin" model, involved making loans and holding them till maturity, enjoying borrowers' interest payments as profit. However, beginning in the 1980s, and even more so in the 1990s, banks shifted to an "originate and distribute," or O&D, model. With O&D, banks issue loans and then pool them together for sale, via the now-notorious securitization process (which we will get to in a moment). The resulting securities offered lots of opportunities for high returns, money came from all over the world to purchase them, and securitization expanded accordingly.

What all this money in the economy meant—or, in Keynesian terms, what all this *liquidity* meant—was that money became one of the easiest assets to get your hands on. There seemed to be a virtually unending supply at unbelievably low prices (interest rates sitting at historic lows). The biggest problem for finance capital, and almost anybody else who wanted to borrow to invest, was not where to get the money, but where to put it all—strange as that may sound to the vast majority of the planet's population, who will never face this "problem." Idle money is not capital; it is not accumulating (Chapter 2). So, people who could get money cheaply were constantly in search of profitable places to invest it. New securities and lending to new consumers proved highly attractive prospects. This helped ramp up prices, especially in real estate but in all asset markets, because it made sense to bid high, knowing money for the purchase was relatively cheap, and banks were eager to lend it. This was also true of new securities themselves, and financial firms and funds borrowed cheaply to buy those up too.

The upshot was a flood of easy money sloshing around and a real estate market in which it looked like nothing could go wrong—prices just rose and rose. Even if you made a bad call and bought something you couldn't afford, or loaned someone money who defaulted, you could still cover your bet and more, since the asset in question seemed guaranteed to exceed the value you paid or loaned for it.[61]

These conditions produced property booms in most of the economies of the global North. From about 2002 to 2006, rising prices and frenzied spending drove the "turn-around" of the traditionally slower-growth, low-wage, less industrialized economies of southern Europe and Ireland, all of which exploded in an unprecedented orgy of new real estate-based riches. Borrowers previously considered too risky became attractive candidates for loans. In the US especially, anybody with a pulse became an attractive candidate for a loan, and some without a pulse. Here lies the story of "subprime" mortgages, the infamous contracts behind the securities that triggered the 2007 crisis.

(2) How Subprime Mortgages Work[62]

For many of us, discussing financial dynamics like mortgage securitization is intimidating. It seems to demand some level of expertise, and the language sounds unfamiliar and technical, and sometimes doesn't seem to make a lot of sense. For example, people sometimes ask

---

61 And to top it all off, in the US, mortgage interest is deducted from income for tax purposes, and upon mortgage default, the creditor has no access to the debtors' other assets.

62 Much of the explanation and examples in this section are drawn from Adam Ashcraft and Til Schuermann's extraordinarily helpful "Understanding the Securitization of Subprime Mortgage Credit," Federal Reserve Bank of New York, Staff Report no. 318 (March 2008).

me why subprime mortgages are bad, since, when they hear "subprime," they tend to think of "prime rate," a base interest rate set by banks. Not without reason, I suppose, they assume a "subprime" loan should have an interest rate even lower than prime, which would indeed be very good, almost unimaginable, from a consumer's perspective. But the prime in subprime does not refer to the interest rate; it refers to the borrowers. A subprime mortgage is subprime because the person borrowing it is subprime, i.e., less than preferable.[63]

It is worth noting that not all of the mortgages behind the assets that crashed in the subprime crisis were in fact technically subprime; they were not all loans to borrowers who fall below certain credit-rating thresholds or debt-to-income ratios. When the press and policy makers talked about the "subprime crisis" in general, other kinds of mortgages were also involved. The most important of these were so-called "Alt-A" (borrowers with higher-than-subprime credit scores, but inadequate documentation or higher debt loads), and "Jumbo" (where a higher proportion of the asset's value is being funded by the loan than is considered "secure"). Although "actual" subprime mortgages were the biggest category of mortgages behind the crisis, these others forms—many with just as elevated interest rates or payment burdens—were (and are) also important.

---

63 Of course, the lenders would not put it that way—they would say it is the credit conditions of the loan that are subprime, not the borrower him or herself—but however much the lender believes it, this "newspeak" is patent Orwellian manipulation. The industry does not really speak of "prime" mortgages; the adjective only comes up in the context of subprime markets.

The key point is that because the borrowers and borrowing conditions are *sub*prime, the interest rates are extremely *super*prime—super-*duper*-prime, even. They consequently impose an extraordinary burden on borrowers, a burden exacerbated by the loan's contractual structure. It is easier to understand this burden if you understand how a conventional mortgage like mine is usually structured. Mortgages are debt contracts backed by real property, and the standard variety has several characteristics. First, they are "fixed-rate" mortgages, or FRMs. With FRMs, monthly payments are fixed over a set period (usually five years), and the interest rate on debt outstanding is readjusted at the end of each period for the life of the loan (usually twenty-five years, but thirty or forty is increasingly common).[64]

Many wealthy capitalist countries have industry-wide regulations or standards that define conventional mortgages by limiting the value of a mortgage according to two main criteria. The first, how much money the household earns, matters as a "rule of thumb." Under non-orgiastic conditions, for example, it is common for banks to limit loan sizes so total monthly debt payments do not exceed approximately one-third of regular household income. The second determinant of the size of a conventional mortgage is a general practice (sometimes legally required, sometimes not): capping the loan at some maximum percentage of the value of the prop-

---

64 As a "prime" borrower you can also get a floating or "variable" rate mortgage, which has similar arrangements for payment and purchase. The difference is that the interest accrued is affected by ongoing shifts in some other market interest rate. But payments are fixed in amount, and the bank just keeps a running tab as to how much you have paid down in interest or principal.

erty. For example, if the maximum loan-to-value ratio is 75 percent, then you need to come up with one quarter of the total cost as a down-payment to put toward purchase. In most cases, the bank can exceed this limit, but often with additional penalty costs and potentially higher interest rates (in US terms, this is a Jumbo mortgage). When my family borrowed from the local credit union to buy a home, we had to come up with a quarter of the cost ourselves to avoid extra debt, and we could only consider houses with prices that kept our mortgage payments below one-third of our total income.

Subprime mortgages are structured very differently. First, they are virtually all "adjustable-rate" mortgages, or ARMs. With a subprime ARM, the mortgage is structured so that for the first two or three years of the loan, the borrower pays a so-called "teaser" interest rate, which, after the preliminary period, adjusts to a level determined by some fluctuating rate on the financial markets (like six-month LIBOR—a key international interbank lending rate) plus a "marginal" or add-on percentage that is fixed for the term of the loan. These mortgages, most of which have a thirty-year duration, are called 2/28 or 3/27 mortgages, the first number being the teaser years, the second the remainder of the loan period at the "adjusted rate" (say, six-month LIBOR + 5 percent). The interest rates in the post-teaser period are readjusted every 6 months, and payments are readjusted on that interval as well. This means the borrower or mortgagor has to re-budget every 6 months to make sure he or she can cover the payments, which often rise to quite a substantial portion of his or her income.

You might think a "teaser" rate would be pretty attractive, perhaps quite low. But given the extent to which subprime borrowers are restricted in their access to credit—they are often in the almost-impossible-to-get-a-loan category—"teaser" rates are nothing to write home about relative to what "prime" borrowers get. For example, in 2006, the teaser rate for subprime borrowers was around 8.6 percent, when central bank rates were about 5.5 percent. As soon as the teaser period is over—a moment called "reset"—rates on these loans rise dramatically, and monthly payments jump accordingly. For example, in a 2/28 ARM, rates around 8 or 9 percent often reset about 12 percent. As a minimal form of borrower protection, there are usually caps on the amount rates can rise in a single six-month period, commonly about 1.5 percent, and there is a ceiling on the interest rate over the life of the loan (15–16 percent), above which it cannot rise. *But,* there is also a floor, usually the teaser rate, below which the loan's interest rate will not drop, even if market rates are lower.

An important result of this arrangement is that at reset, expenses go up a great deal—in the example I have been using (a "real" subprime mortgage), the household's monthly payments rose by 15 percent after two years, and by another 12 percent six months later. If the borrower originally committed to mortgage payments that demanded 40 percent of monthly income, then two-and-a-half years into the loan, she or he will owe monthly payments amounting to more than half of income (assuming real income and the base market interest rate stays around the same level as at the time of purchase). In other words, there is no need for the borrower's wages to fall or interest rates to rise to rapidly make the loan untenable. It is structured to become extraordinarily burdensome, and fast—there is no need for bad luck or volatility. To top it all off, the loan I am describing is among the better in the subprime category. There are worse arrangements. In one, the first five years are interest-only payments, which means that reset at the five-year mark raises payments enormously. In another, the payments are amortized over forty years, to keep them low, but are scheduled on a thirty-year payback, meaning the homeowner had to have 120 months of cash at the end of the mortgage to cover the remaining debt (a so-called "balloon" payment).

Ultimately, there are three features to note about the structure of these debts:

> (a) Unlike FRMs, the ARM borrower bears almost all the interest rate risk. In conventional mortgages, at least over the (optional) five-year fixed-rate periods, the lender bears the interest rate risk; if market rates skyrocket tomorrow, mine stays the same, at least until renegotiation. In a subprime mortgage it is adjusted every six months.

> (b) Unless the borrower's income rises substantially during the teaser period, there is a good chance the increased payments after reset will be unaffordable. The only way to deal with this additional monthly burden (aside from defaulting, as so many did) is to sell the property and repay the loan (with prepayment penalties), or to refinance the mortgage (renegotiate the payment schedule and rate if possible).

> (c) The only way these loans make sense, especially given the probability of default after reset, is if housing prices rise continually. If they

fall, then selling the property, or refinancing, will not cover the loan, and the borrower will have "negative equity," lose his or her property, and the lender will probably lose money on the loan.

(3) How these Mortgages Entered the Financial System, or "Securitization"

These mortgage and real estate dynamics have come to matter a lot in recent years. These loans are not merely some shadowy sideshow contracts between predatory lenders and "financially unsophisticated" borrowers at the margins of modern capitalism. The lenders include both shifty mortgage brokers and established (but perhaps no less shifty) commercial banks, and the loans themselves are an important object of the "securitization" process that lies at the heart of modern, financialized neoliberalism.

Securitization, as mentioned earlier, is a process through which flows of funds (like monthly mortgage payments) are turned into transferable assets. More precisely, it is how loans leave the hands of the lenders (where they would have stayed in the old "net margin" banking model), are purchased and used to issue into debt securities—circulating financial assets that are purchased and sold by investors in financial markets. Not only are these securities transferable on the market, they are part of an effort to off-load the risk taken by the lender. At this level, the process is reasonably straightforward, but in practice it can demand computational wizardry and organizational capacity.

The practical side of mortgage securitization involves five main steps.[65] First, the lender, or "originator,"

---

65 Mortgage securitization is ongoing; it did not end with the subprime crisis.

loans money to borrowers (the people actually purchasing a home). This debt contract is the mortgage proper. The originator then pools mortgages together in a portfolio (containing, on average 3000 to 4000 mortgages), which it sells, as a unit, to an "arranger" or "issuer." An arranger wants to own a portfolio of thousands of mortgages because whoever holds a mortgage receives the debtor's monthly payments. If you own a portfolio of 3500 mortgages, each of which owes on average $1500 monthly, then you receive $5.25 million dollars in payments every month, if the debtors don't default.

Leading up to the collapse of the subprime market, such loan-pooling was not difficult. While there were many small lenders involved in subprime mortgage lending, a substantial portion of loan origination (the "O" in O&D banking) was undertaken by very large financial firms, or arms of such firms, some of which have since vanished from the face of the Earth (e.g., Washington Mutual or New Century Financial). The size of the many these firms allowed them to make enormous numbers of loans, which they could pool together "in-house," and then sell for a profit. For example, a portfolio of 3500 loans valued at $100 million, based on the income flows from 3500 households' monthly payments, might be sold to an arranger for $102 million.

Second, the arranger (usually a firm) who buys the portfolio creates what is called a "bankruptcy-remote" trust, a wholly owned but legally separate entity housed with a "trustee," generally a big commercial bank. The trust "purchases" the package of mortgages. The arranger—often but not only an investment bank like Goldman Sachs—is doing this complicated institutional and

legal dance because it does not want to carry the mortgage risk anymore than the originator. The trust is legally structured so that if it goes bankrupt because the borrowers default (for instance), the investors who bought
the loan portfolio do not go down with it.

Now, the arranger had to pay the originator millions of dollars for the original portfolio, money it obviously cannot recoup until the deal has been finalized
and the securities issued and sold. If the arranger is a big
financial firm, they can cover the costs themselves while
everything is sewn up. But many arrangers, sometimes
even big firms, cover those costs by borrowing from a
firm called a "warehouse lender," which lends against the
value of the mortgages as collateral.[66] This loan usually
requires a "haircut" or "over-collateralization": the warehouse lender demands collateral posted against the loan
worth more than the loan itself. This is how a warehouse
lender attempts to guarantee itself a profit if the arranger
defaults. Given the institutional and contractual structure of the loan, however, it turned out to be ineffective,
since when the arranger failed to repay the loan during
the crisis, it was due to a collapse in the value of the collateral (the mortgage portfolio). It is precisely this accumulation of risk on an inadequate material basis that led
to the cascade of failure when the portfolios did begin
to "underperform."

---

66 "Collateral" describes any asset used to "secure" a loan. It is the
stuff the borrower agrees to forfeit to the lender in the event
of default. This is the same principle behind pawnshops: you
bring in your bicycle, the pawnbroker lends you money, and
if you don't repay the loan and interest, the pawnbroker keeps
the bicycle. A mortgage is distinguished by the fact that the
"collateral" is not something you already own, but the property
purchased with the loan.

Third, the arranger then initiates the process of securitization proper, i.e., going through the steps involved in issuing securities, the value of which is "backed" by the loan portfolio. This is why the securities that became notorious during the crisis were called "mortgage-backed" or "asset-backed" securities (MBSs or ABSs). These steps are largely administrative or institutional: obtaining credit ratings for the securities to be issued; hiring, if necessary, experts to structure the deal from a legal and accounting perspective (this is what investment banks specialize in); covering the costs associated with issuing the securities; filing with the necessary regulators, etc. This is all worth the arranger's time because it receives fees for such services, charged to the purchasers of the securities, and its profit is the value of the securities at sale, less the amount originally paid for the portfolio of loans and the costs of arranging.

Fourth, the trust, which legally holds the mortgages, hires a "servicer" to make sure the mortgagors make their payments. The servicer is paid a monthly fee based on the value of loans outstanding. Here, however, we run up against one of the more glaring principal-agent problems in a process packed with them. The servicer clearly has an incentive to keep the mortgages in the portfolio from being repaid, because its fee is based on the value of debts outstanding. So the trust usually hires a "master servicer" to monitor the servicer. (You might be forgiven for thinking this could become a bit of a joke: who monitors the master servicer? The headmaster servicer! And the lord headmaster servicer monitors the headmaster …) This is only another example of the way in which all sorts of other considerations beyond supply and demand enter into contracting and pricing.

Fifth, the securities are finally issued, or put on the market, and purchased by "asset managers" (pension fund managers, hedge fund managers etc.) who are acting for their funds' investors. The firms involved in arranging may sometimes keep some of the securities for themselves, or sell them to another arm of the firm. But whichever financial firm or trader comes to hold these securities will buy and sell them in an attempt to maximize the value of their "assets under management."

You might be wondering what the end-product of this process, the securities themselves, are exactly. What do they look like? How do they work? If they can provide a return to an investor, how does that work? These securities, like all the complex financial instruments designed over the last couple of decades, are the outcome of well-remunerated computational and organizational creativity, involving "innovative" rethinking of everything from the tax code to mathematical models. Much of the wizardry happens with the arranger. Take Goldman Sachs, for example. As an arranger, Goldman will create a "bankruptcy-remote" trust that is essentially one big pile of mortgages. With our hypothetical 3500–mortgage pool, the trust has a potential monthly income of $5.25 million. That is a lot of money.

In the financial world, an anticipated and consistent flow of income in the future is an "asset," and its value is based on the volume of the flow and the risk that all or some of it might dry up, temporarily or permanently. The larger the future flow, and the more a "sure thing" it appears, the more valuable it is as an asset *in the present*. This is the same principle a bank relies on when it lends you money for big-ticket items you do not presently have the capacity to purchase without the loan. The bank considers your monthly income, assesses its level and how steady it is likely to be in the future, and considers that future income your "asset" in the present. This anticipated income, which you will use to repay the bank, is the basis upon which the bank decides if lending you the money is or is not a good idea. Similarly, with the portfolio of mortgages, Goldman's trust has an asset whose value depends on (a) a potential monthly income of $5.25 million; and (b) the likely level of expected or "actually realized" income (which, given defaults, late payments, and other complications, will never be 100 percent).

In the financial world, you can do one of three things with an asset. You can hold it, and enjoy the income associated with holding it (in this case, the monthly mortgage payments). You can sell it, as you would your bicycle or your car. Or, you can borrow money against it, treating it as collateral: you might say to your friend, "If you lend me $400, I will pay you back in a year, with interest. If I don't, you can have my bicycle, which is worth $425,"[67] In our example, Goldman owns a (potentially) valuable asset in the pool of mortgages, which if it does not choose to hold on to, it can just plain sell—which might *still* involve securitization—or it can borrow against it. If it chooses the latter, then it will issue "securities" as the means to do that borrowing. This is the key moment of "financial innovation." Goldman, the arranger, issues debt securities (structurally similar to bonds) backed by its asset, a flow of mortgage payments that is, for all intents and purposes, a constant money-producing tube. Just as in the cases of Brazil and Canada discussed in Chapter 5, it borrows money from

---

67 This is an example of over-collateralization.

investors by selling bonds promising a yield it, and pre-sumably the investors, believes it can deliver.

The bonds in this case are the asset-backed or mort-gage-backed securities we hear so much about. Investors purchase asset-backed securities because the promised yield is worth the investment. The higher the risk as-sociated with the security, the higher the yield or inter-est rate the arranger/issuer promises to pay the investor. Goldman's motivation for issuing the securities lies not solely in the additional profits it hopes to earn with the sale of the securities. If it simply keeps the asset on hand to enjoy the income flow, it is bearing the risks associ-ated with the loans all by itself. It—or more precisely, its "bankruptcy-remote" trust—is the loser if people de-fault. So it issues securities both to make a profit (via fees and price markups) and to spread the risk. (Investment bankers like to say "distribute" the risk, since they see their primary social function, the "good" they do in the world, as that of "distributing" risk to those who can bear it. We can see now how well this works, and how valuable this "social function" is. In practice, it is merely a variation on "privatize the gains, socialize the losses.")

One of the reasons for spreading the risk of sub-prime mortgage default to investors is that it is, in fact, highly likely. After following the steps in subprime mortgage securitization, it is easy to forget that the pool of debts consists of high interest loans made to many who are not likely to manage the payments very easily. This means that the assets "backing" the secu-rities may not appear all that secure to investors. The problem for the arranger is thus how to get investors to buy securities that look like they could turn to ashes at a moment's notice.

The solution to this problem is to "structure" the financial instruments (the securities) associated with the underlying asset. "Structured" finance is one of the most important "developments" in the history of "financial innovation." It involves issuing securities divided into "tranches" (French for "slices") ranked in terms of the certainty their holders will receive payouts. In other words, each tranche contains securities to which a relative level of risk is attached. For any pool of mortgages, a range of different securities is issued, some marked as low risk, some medium, some high. Lowest-risk securities earn the lowest rates of interest, highest-risk earn the highest.

How, you may wonder, with a pool of three or four thousand basically similar mortgages, can you issue securities with different risks and returns? This is how: the arranger structures the securities so that the lowest-risk ones are considered low risk because they are the first to receive their payments on schedule. If there is a problem with the flow of funds from the money-tube, and only enough comes in to cover thee-quarters of the issuer's debt payments, then those holding the highest-yielding (but riskiest) quarter of the securities don't receive payment. The lowest-risk tranches are called "senior," the middle are called "mezzanine," and the highest-risk, nicknamed "toxic waste" in the industry, are—in a sort of perverse inside joke—called "equity" tranches. Who doesn't want some "equity?" Oh, I'll take some of that, yes, please.

From the perspective of finance capital (which includes the issuer and the investor or security-purchaser), the most important part of the "innovation" in structuring is the mathematical modeling that "proves" its

sound business sense. Worked out by financial economists, computer scientists, and other financial industry
"quants," that modeling demonstrates that *if* the risk
of default among the mortgages in the pool is uncorrelated—i.e., it is statistically unlikely that a substantial
proportion will default at the same time—then even
though the individual loans themselves are very risky,
those holding the lowest risk, "senior" securities will
likely be paid. Indeed, the modeling, with the help of
very compliant and enormously powerful credit-rating
agencies, allowed issuers to classify a large part of the
securities as senior, and they consequently received quite
a high credit rating.

This credit rating matters a great deal, because the
structuring of subprime mortgage-backed securities allowed firms to sell the securities to many financial market participants who otherwise would not have risked it,
or who would have been legally prevented from doing
so. For example, many pension fund managers are barred
from buying assets that are not "investment grade" (at
least an "A" rating by the credit agencies). Without the
"structuring" process, it would be absolutely impossible
for these securities to be rated highly enough to circulate
so widely and in such volumes. But structuring is a way
of turning BBB loans into AAA-rated securities, with
the help of credit agencies who are paid by the arrangers
to "rate" the securities.

(4) The Blow-Up (or Meltdown) and Capitalism

We all know where this wound up—and how it
continues to spin out of control. In truth, the "financial innovation" got quite a bit more complicated than I
have related here. Of several features I have not covered

in detail, one might mention credit default swaps, or CDSs. A CDS is essentially an insurance contract covering losses associated with the premature end of payments on a financial asset. Just as in other insurance contracts, one party agrees to pay a regular fee, equivalent to a small fraction of the value of the security. In return, the counterparty insures the value of the security in the event that it fails to bring in the anticipated payments. Moreover—and this often shocks us nonfinanciers, as it should—finance capitalists freely write CDS contracts for securities they do not even own. In other words, and this is not at all uncommon, they can own the rights to insurance payouts for assets they do not hold. This is opportunism turned up to eleven, and in the months following the subprime collapse in 2007–2008, many firms intentionally drove down certain markets to force their own CDS payouts. CDSs greatly exacerbated the effects of the market's implosion, since they grossly multiplied the number of securities whose value depended upon the underlying asset-base. American Insurance Group (AIG), perhaps the single biggest player in the CDS market, had to be bailed out by the US government to the tune of more than $120 billion dollars.

Subprime-based financial instruments multiplied (for example, "interest rate swaps," transferable securities that allowed financiers to switch the interest rate that determined an asset's returns from fixed-rate to variable, were also used throughout the process). So much so that the value of circulating securities increased exponentially as financial firms doubled, and sometimes tripled, the complexity by repeating the pooling process, this time using the asset-backed securities themselves, as opposed to the original mortgages. These pools were then structured into so-called collateralized debt obligations (CDOs), with securities issued just like the first time around. The resulting income was then reinvested in more such securities, and so on. The dynamic seemed to have no meaningful limits.

All of these securities are basically different types of derivatives, in the sense that they are derived from the value of an original asset—in this case, the money coming in from a pool of mortgage payments. The problem is, like the subprime business on which it was precariously balanced, the whole structure was premised on rising real estate prices and low and uncorrelated default rates: if a borrower could not pay their mortgage, they could sell their home for more than what they paid for it, repay the lender, and the process could start again.

Then, in February 2007, subprime mortgage defaults started to increase, a couple of mortgage originators went under, and everyone started to get a bit nervous. The models that promised the impossibility of correlated mass default no longer seemed accurate descriptions of reality. By July and August, it was getting hard to sell the securities associated with the mortgages, be they MBSs, CDSs, CDOs or any other ladle-full of alphabet soup. Mortgage originators and arrangers were left holding enormous piles of risky loans—borrowers defaulted by the thousands and they carried the risk. Many went bankrupt. Poof!

Then all hell broke loose. Securities issuers had to start selling what they had on their hands, just to pay people clamouring for the money they were promised when purchasing the securities. But selling *en masse* only drove down prices further, so the fire-sales earned asset holders less and less. To make matters worse, it is common practice in finance to write contracts (and securities are debtor-creditor contracts) that stipulate that when the value of the security drops below a pre-determined threshold, the issuer has either to pay the debt-holders higher yield, or to put up more collateral. But the issuers, in this case investment banks and others, had panic-sold most of their even remotely valuable assets, and thus could neither pay the debt-holders nor post more collateral.

On top of that, when they tried to "unwind" the mortgage-backed securities, and get back to the underlying assets—the real estate—to which they now had some legal claim (since the home-purchasers had defaulted), it proved enormously, even impossibly, complicated. In any one pool thousands of mortgages were spread all over the US. If you were a German bank, for example, the distance only created additional obstacles to figuring this out. And this leaves aside that a lot of the real estate wasn't worth much anyway, consisting as it did of properties suffering from plummeting housing prices and an unprecedented supply glut, much of it in previously (and now once more) less-than-"desirable" locales like the suburbs of the US South and Midwest. It turned out that the models were useless, "correlation" was in fact more than possible, and simultaneous default on a colossal scale was a reality.

Those holding credit default swaps called their counterparties to demand payment. Most of the counterparties, like AIG, had spent the money they made from CDS payments on more of the same and other asset-backed securities. They were not even close to being able to meet their obligations without selling what they had. But much of what they had was absolutely worthless—literally *worthless*: not "of considerably less value," but of no value at all. What was worth something they put up for sale on markets now flooded with similar assets, which of course pushed prices into the abyss, and the spiral accelerated.

By mid-2008, major financial institutions like the Wall Street investment bank Bear Stearns were going under, and the US government stepped in to contain a potential meltdown. Other firms were teetering, many of them large. But the scale of what was to come only became visible in September, when the Treasury and the Fed made the fateful decision to let Lehman Brothers, an elite financial goliath of Wall Street, go down. In so doing, they actually let their orthodoxy prove its worth by allowing something like the "free market" to do its work in the financial sector. The result, from the perspective of capital at least, was catastrophe. Market indexes across the world, already shaky, dropped off a cliff. In allowing Lehman to fail—which, as fun as it was to watch in a "chickens coming home to roost" way, hurt a lot of innocent working people very badly—the US government called the bluff of financiers playing the moral hazard game. The conservative right that has since coagulated as the Tea Party loved it. But as problematic as the opportunistic risk-taking of these massive firms was, Lehman's collapse also suggested that if worse came to worst, there was no guarantee the state would step in—the one thing that always stood behind the financial house of cards, in good times and in bad.

By late 2008, there was hardly a single player or firm in global finance that was not worried they were about to go under, and everyone was terrified that any fund or individual or bank to whom they loaned money to was about to collapse under the weight of its debts. As a result, no one would lend to anyone, and the liquidity that so recently soaked the economy dried up almost entirely. Everyone fretted they might lend money today to a bank that would be bankrupt tomorrow, or buy the corporate bonds (or "paper") of a firm moments away from bankruptcy. Mortgage loans even for the most "credit-worthy" borrowers were restricted, and banks held back on the interbank market that is the key to the everyday function of the monetary system. This is how the "subprime crisis" turned into the "credit crunch." The state, having learned the Lehman lesson, then stepped in aggressively. With the help of Ivy League economists who quickly and conveniently forgot that the crisis was supposed to be impossible according to policy "wisdom" they had been flogging for two decades, the state identified firms considered "too big too fail" (like AIG), and frantically propped them up with whatever they could muster. Treasuries found buckets of money that for some reason only months before had been impossible to find for schools or health care. Central banks cut interest rates to unprecedented lows, pumped money into the banking system, accepted almost anything as collateral against massive low-interest loans to the financial sector, and took virtual ownership of major institutions.[68]

---

68 A lot of these efforts focused on getting "toxic" assets off financial firms' balance sheets so they could "recapitalize"—i.e., look sound enough on paper to borrow money again. To this end, the state took possession of much of the alphabet-soup assets. The ABSs, CDOs, etc. did not just disappear, as it sometimes seems. They are still there, their risks being borne by the public sector, in the hope that one day the markets will revive and the state will be able to unload them.

If there is one thing all of this makes clear, it is that this (increasingly frequent) kind of crisis is a product of capitalism. Capitalism, at least to this point in human history, is the only mode of production that makes this possible. And it is precisely those aspects of capitalism that make it such an organizational wonder historically—its decentralized mechanisms, its profit imperative, its competitiveness—that also make it prone to crises. Capitalism's tendency to incorporate things that once hindered it, to integrate economic relations more and more tightly—often via monetary or financial mechanisms—end up making it likely, when one car tips, that the whole train will derail. To the extent that neoliberalism involves the systematic prioritization of precisely these features of capitalism, to the naïve neglect of political and economic stabilization and legitimation, this roller coaster gets more and more crazy over time, its "ups" lifting fewer people with each climb.

Whether we can have a capitalism that is not defined by these characteristics remains unknown; we cannot say what the future holds. History, however, suggests it is highly unlikely, even if we leave aside (as capitalists prefer) looming environmental and/or social catastrophe—which seems unwise. I am not inclined to press our luck on this front.

7

Disassembly Required, or, This Will Not Be Easy

The meltdown that began with the subprime collapse in the US will mark an important phase in the history of capitalism. Of that we can be sure. For while the crisis is in many ways the condensation of the last four decades of global capitalism, as representative of modern capital's function as the exhilarating bubbles that preceded it, it would be wrong to suggest that nothing has changed. A great deal has changed, although it is not clear how much, where, or how long it will last. The nuts-and-bolts objectives and policy measures of market über-fundamentalism, the global "how-to" manual for economic development only a few short years before, were aggressively challenged in the wake of the crisis. While there were a few who saw the writing on the wall, for those surfing the neoliberal wave, all those unquestionably sound means to vast riches suddenly seemed, well, highly questionable. Even in the hallowed halls of orthodox capitalist reason—the US Treasury, central banks, and Ivy League economics departments—the truth seemed much less true. Some on the left even began to talk about the "end of neoliberalism," and even now, five years later, a dwindling few still do.

Alas, at least as I write, it has not come to pass. After some brief moments of semi-delirious soul-searching, unsettled champions of neoliberalism rediscovered their faith and reasserted the revealed truth of the doctrine that enriched them. Indeed, despite the rage boiling in streets and plazas around the world, the main ideologues and beneficiaries of neoliberalization managed, amazingly, to spin the collapse they precipitated into a story about the profligate irresponsibility and unrealistic expectations of workers, students, and the unemployed. The massive holes in every capitalist nation's public and private finances were perfunctorily redefined as the result of popular desire to "live beyond our means," from which the masses must be weaned once and for all. The answer elites proposed, and proceeded to impose, looked a lot like an IMF structural adjustment plan—austerity, privatization, liberalization—with an emphasis on *austerity*, a program of vicious cuts in public subsidies and state retrenchment designed and managed by exactly the same individuals and institutions who created the crises in the first place.

From what I can tell, those in charge seem to have honestly convinced themselves with this disturbing act of historical revisionism. Not that there is no duplicity; there are many financiers who have worked tirelessly to disavow responsibility for events and processes they know are their fault. But at the level of capitalist governance and reason, it seems a couple of sleepless nights functioned as a sort of confessional, after which neoliberal logic and faith reasserted itself (which makes sense, since logic and faith justify each other). Indeed, to listen to Euro-American austeritites talk, you would think austerity is how capitalists say the rosary, a market-imposed penance for "our" sins.

Yet it may turn out that our current moment is eventually seen as the high-water mark of such powerful illusions, and the authority of their missionaries. In Europe, at least, where the whole continent has been rocked by a crisis for which its capitalists and governments cannot escape some blame (despite their efforts to pin it on the US and the UK), the politics of austerity have reached a breaking point. This is especially so in the member nations of the European Union or EU, and to an even greater degree in the Eurozone, the group of members who share a single currency.

While a full account of European dynamics in relation to the financial crisis is impossible here, clearly the global meltdown has left the EU and its member states reeling.[69] As of 2013, the principal challenge facing European capitalism is to maintain the political economic stability of a union in which the effects of economic crisis are remarkably uneven. At its institutional core, this is a crisis of the financial system—a crisis of the essential circulatory system of contemporary capitalism—and the banking systems of southern Europe (and Ireland) in particular have been hammered. Yet it is not that German and French bankers are somehow "smarter" finance capitalists. The southern nation-states (the so-called "PIIGS": Portugal, Ireland, Italy, Greece, and Spain) have private financial institutions no more stupid or

---

69 For the full story, see Costas Lapavitsas' *Crisis in the Eurozone* (London: Verso, 2012), and for a helpful introduction to the relevant terminology, see the glossary in the *Guardian*, 1 June 2012, http://www.guardian.co.uk/business/2012/jun/01/eurozone-glossary.

myopic than banks in Germany or France (or the UK or North America, for that matter). As the preceding chapters show, it is not historically unprecedented stupidity or greed that leads to capitalism's crises. This financial crisis—the latest in a long and increasingly frequent series—is a product of capitalism's *systemic* dynamics. This is where it leads, over and over again, from Cracow to Cleveland, Cape Town to Copenhagen. Not to suggest these nations' elites are blameless, of course, but the fact that banks' actions produced worse outcomes for the PIIGS than for other EU members is not due to exceptionally poor judgment, but to typical, if severe, capitalist crisis unfolding in the context of macroeconomic and political institutions much less robust than those of their northern neighbours.

That there are many historically entrenched reasons for this relative fragility does not make the problems any less painful for southern Europeans. I write these paragraphs in a café in Spain, and the crisis, and Madrid's (mis)management of it, is the topic of almost every conversation around me. It is on every newspaper's front page, day after day. It is, in the crudely dispassionate academic phrase, a "fascinating time to be here." In Vancouver, where I live and work, the social and political wastes laid by capitalism's financialized neoliberal variety are much less readily evident, at least so far.

In Spain, however, with official unemployment at 25 percent (in reality it is significantly higher), 50 percent among those under 25 years old, and both expected to rise, there is no way to miss it—even in the relative affluence of Catalunya, where I am. Except in the immigrant-filled towers and impoverished suburbs of Barcelona (the capital), the crisis has bitten less hard here than in the rest of the country. Catalunya has a relatively developed, industrialized economy that is by no means representative of Spain. The province nurses regionally-based grievances, many quite justifiable, mixed as they are with the legacy of Franco and his murderous attempt to obliterate the Catalan identity and language to repay the region (especially Barcelona) for its resistance during the Spanish Civil War (1936–39). But one of the more powerful variations on regionalism at present is founded in Catalans' longstanding vision of Catalunya as the progressive, modern, most "European" part of Spain. Its average income is higher, its agriculture more productive, its cities more cosmopolitan, its economy more industrialized, and—at least according to many Catalans— its citizens harder-working and more entrepreneurial. Spain's federal structure thus means Catalunya tends to contribute more in taxes to the national budget than flow back its way, and crisis has exacerbated the bitterness born of this "unfairness." As far as many Catalans are concerned, despite the fact that it has the largest debts of all Spanish regions, both absolutely and relative to its economy, Catalunya would not be in this mess if it were not bound to unproductive laggards in the rest of Spain, especially to poor regions like Andalucía, Murcia, and Extremadura in the south, and the parasitic state apparatus in Madrid. This, more than love of *la nació catalana*, is arguably the main force that put 1.5 million people in the streets of Barcelona in September 2012, and, two weeks later, energized the 100,000 fans chanting "*Independència!*" before the kick-off at FC Barcelona's tense derby against Franco's beloved Real Madrid.[70]

---

70 See the Assemblea Nacional Catalana's "Manifest de la Marxa cap a la Independència" [Manifesto of the March for Indepen-

It is not only Spain's regional differentiation that reminds us of the multiple ways capitalist crisis can propagate. Spain is also politically instructive for anticapitalists, both within and outside Spanish borders, because it is ensnared in what is essentially a macroscopic wageworker's bind. This is not to suggest the Spanish state or Spanish people "really" want out of capitalism, nor that other countries like Greece are not similarly entangled. Rather, from whatever political angle people struggle to surmount its political and economic impasses, Spain is for all intents and purposes trapped. According to capitalism's logic, there is literally no way out—and outside of it, there is fear of the punishment that is sure to follow. Certainly, there is much self-interest, profiteering, and gendered and racialized power at work in the politics of the moment, but at a broad social and institutional level, it is paralysis that dominates, because the only "choice" is not a choice. The untenable status quo demands the consideration of radical options, yet those very options are written off as unimaginable. What is obviously necessary appears just as obviously impossible—the risks seem too high, even in the eyes of many who whole-heartedly identify with the left (who make up a greater proportion of the population than in North America or the UK).

This argument requires a bit of context. Most of the attention Spain's current instability receives is due to its membership in the Eurozone monetary union. The shared currency, the euro, was in many ways a necessary product of post–World War II western European capitalist development. Cooperation among Europe's liberal

dence], http://marxa.assemblea.cat/sites/default/files/pictures/manifest_marxa.pdf.

democracies began decades ago, and a smaller and much less powerful version of the EU emerged as early as the 1950s. Increasing continental integration and interdependence then led to a series of gradual expansions in membership, and ultimately to the Maastricht Treaty of February 1992, the basis of the EU as it exists today. Spain was one of twelve original signatories of the treaty, which formally gave the EU some features traditionally associated with nation-states: its own (rather weak) parliament and executive (the European Commission) based in Brussels, and (in 1998) its own central bank, the most "independent" central bank in the world, headquartered in Frankfurt.[71] Not that Maastricht founded a union of equals. On the contrary, the EU is anchored in, and beholden to, the relative economic and political power of France and, even more so, Germany.

From the perspective of capital and western Europe's largely neoliberal political leadership, the whole point of Maastricht was to create the conditions for monetary union in the EU, a goal realized six years later, on 1 January 1999.[72] Not all members of the EU joined the currency union. The UK, the most notable exception, negotiated a way to stay in the EU while remaining outside the so-called "Eurozone." Greece, who joined the EU in 1981, is the only nation of those now lumped together in the PIIGS barred from adopting the euro in 1999. It had to wait until 2001 because it did not meet minimum macroeconomic stability or "convergence" criteria.

---

71 On the significance of central bank "independence" for contemporary capitalism, see Chapters 3 and 5.

72 At first, the euro only existed "electronically," for the financial system. The physical form of the currency went into circulation on 1 January 2002.

These minimum criteria for entry into the Eurozone echo the criteria for EU membership stipulated by the Maastricht Treaty, and they are based on firmly neoliberal principles. The qualifications nation-states needed to sign Maastricht were determined entirely by what orthodox economics identified as the demands of monetary union. Orthodox macroeconomic theory comes in several formally distinct flavours—new classical macro, real business cycle theory, new neoclassical synthesis— but all claim to prove the effectiveness of the same basic policies, because all are built on monetarist foundations. According to this line of thinking, the essential requirements of monetary union seemed obvious: strictly controlled state spending, minimal inflation, and the complete deregulation of capital flows. The idea, which now looks like a cruel joke, was that productivity differentials across Eurozone members would motivate "liberated" capital to move to take advantage of higher profits. If, for example, some parts of the Eurozone had lower wages than others, than investment would flow into those parts to enjoy the higher returns. This was supposed to continue until competition between capitalists produced a Eurozone-wide equilibrium in which all those opportunities had been "used up," and the entire zone had "converged" on a fiscal, monetary, and profit-rate standard. This mythology put us in the frying pan of the crisis, a contribution one might expect would have discredited it entirely. But it is not dead. Despite the now obvious and potentially catastrophic errors to which it leads, it is also the "logic" that legitimates the leap into the fire of austerity. Many of the same people who flogged it before 2007–08 remain committed to it, and are now using it to tell Europe's middle and working classes to jump into the flames. (They are supposed to go first, to test the temperature.)

When it comes to monetary regimes, twenty-first-century capital is rigidly inflexible. If there is a realm in which contemporary neoliberal capital demands absolute power, it is the realm of money. EU membership thus demanded what are essentially variations on the conditions the IMF imposes on client states: inflation and long-term interest rates near that of the average of the best performers in the Union (i.e., very low), government deficits no higher than 3 percent and debt no higher than 60 percent of the previous year's GDP, and no recent history of currency devaluation. Minimal inflation, little government spending or borrowing, credibility on the international bond markets—and no recent slips in commitment to this neoliberal credo.

As emphasized in several of the previous chapters, the euro-based currency regime to which the EU led was thoroughly neoliberal insofar as it is perhaps the most audacious attempt yet to make monetary policy and money markets the preeminent instrument of political power and capitalist governance. If money is the blood of capitalism's body, the euro created a situation in which a healthy European circulatory system necessitated the end of "traditional" state sovereignty in eleven nation-states. (The number is fourteen if you include western Europe's feudal residue: Monaco, San Marino, and the Vatican, whose currencies were mere tourist souvenirs, tied to the French and Italian anyway).[73] Obviously, some were giv-

---

73 The originals were Austria, Belgium, Finland, France, Germany, Ireland, Italy, Luxembourg, the Netherlands, Portugal, and Spain. Since 1999, six additional countries have adopted the euro: Cyprus, Estonia, Greece, Malta, Slovakia, and Slovenia.

ing up more than others—there are many who would say monetary union gave Germany (and to a lesser extent France) control of monetary matters in all of western Europe—but for the PIIGS at least, monetary union meant the surrender of domestic monetary authority.[74]

In short, Maastricht was a neoliberal package for Europe, one much easier to adopt in the north than in the south. Note, for example, the way the convergence criteria are measured relative to the performance of the most stable and least indebted members, the core northern model economies. Macroeconomic "convergence" did not mean "meeting in the middle." It meant that poorer nation-states had to start acting like rich ones, even if they weren't rich. The treaty was intended to pave the way, and guarantee a commitment to, a monetary regime that finance and big capital saw as necessary and (their theory told them) profitable. It would be naïve to believe that Germany or France or the Netherlands would have willingly yoked themselves to the economic fortunes of the historically "corrupt" and "underperforming" political economies of places like Greece or the Iberian peninsula if it were not reasonably certain, according to the logic of capitalist reason, that this was the best way to realize necessary "efficiencies" and associated "returns." If it were not in line with capitalist imperatives, it would have been unthinkable.[75]

---

74 The states of the Eurozone retained their own central banks as part of the European System of Central Banks (ESCB, founded at the same time as the ECB), but with drastically reduced authority and jurisdiction.

75 Northern European conservatives still resent the way these countries "burgled their way" into the EU. To them, political economic union with the south seemed like political, economic and social suicide (remember that southern Europeans are

The reasons these fears did not win the day lie in the decades preceding the monetary union, an era of increasing interdependence via the institutionalization of "common markets." The persistent instability of diverse moneys and forms of monetary authority across member nations threatened the integrated trade and financial regime consolidated during the 1970s and 1980s. Persistent differentials in inflation rates and returns on capital were particularly irksome. Consequently, the euro and the establishment of the ECB—again, the most independent central bank on Earth—is proof that the kind of non-democratic capitalist monetary authority discussed in Chapter 3 is so essential to the health of modern capitalist states that many of them conceded power over a substantial part of what defines the nation-state as a state. The contradictory combination of commercial integration and monetary fragmentation demanded monetary union, despite northern fears of southern profligacy—fears that now seem confirmed, at least in the eyes of many.

Yet the processes that led Spain and other countries to this point are, from the perspective of the ideas and concepts laid out in Part I, entirely understandable. In the decade following the adoption of the euro, Spain was not immune to the same speculative frenzy that infected the US and the rest of western Europe at the same time. Its banks, with the full and enthusiastic en-

often "racially" subordinated in Europe, similar to the way in which African Americans are positioned in the US; they are coded as lazy, dishonest, and biologically inferior, even and sometimes most in their own countries). See Alain Minc, "An Open Letter to My Friends, the Financiers of America," *New York Review of Books*, volume 56, number 16 (25 October 2012).

dorsement of its regional and national governments, and the rest of the EU powers, were allowed to roam more and more freely in credit and other markets, taking on riskier obligations less and less proportional to their own capital bases. In these historically low-income regions, the new prosperity brought higher wages and increased spending. Spanish residents and firms were encouraged to go big or go home on loans, big-ticket purchases, acquisitions, and expansions, at home and abroad. Foreign financial institutions, awash in so much cash they had no idea what to do with it all, leaped into Spanish bond markets, eagerly snapping up sovereign and corporate debt. The wealthy of the UK and western Europe, and the elites of newly-capitalist eastern Europe, flooded its property markets with money chasing beach-front condos and hillside villas.[76] Personal and corporate incomes and national and regional budgets in Spain were as blissfully and ignorantly dependent upon the extension of the mania as elsewhere.

But the big differences that never really disappeared (and some say were intentionally papered over to justify the monetary union) resurfaced when the crisis hit. Like the other members of the PIIGS club, Spain was relatively underdeveloped in many of those dimensions that have historically anchored the capitalist mode of production. Its domestic markets and industries had less to fall back on, its financial-regulatory system was less sophisticated, its economy was more dependent upon foreign investment, real estate, and tourism, and its political institutions—like the unusual fiscal independence enjoyed

---

76 Even in the depth of the crisis, in the windows of Spanish real estate agencies, the second language of luxury property listings is Russian.

by *comunidades autónomas* like Catalunya and Andalucía—rendered it structurally less prepared to manage the crisis than wealthy fellow Eurozoners to the north.

The Spanish central government bailed out, nationalized, and otherwise coddled the bankers—just as every other capitalist state did after 2007, and just as it was told it must, to avoid becoming a capitalist oxymoron: an economy without banks. This meant digging a debt-hole Spain has neither political nor economic capacity to refill. Particularly problematic are newly risen labour costs, which mean it cannot compete with northern EU countries in export or import markets. For the introduction of monetary union and increased labour mobility via Maastricht has produced—just as German capital planned—a downward wage "convergence" for workers in the traditionally high-wage German labour market. German wage deflation, in combination with a weak euro, has thus exacerbated the competitive advantage Germany enjoyed when the euro was introduced: not only are its labour costs diminished, but its exports are cheaper for foreign buyers. For Spain, without its pre-crisis income flows, there is no way either private or state sector reserves can cover the losses taken to save the banks. And what money or cost-cutting is possible has not been forthcoming, because Madrid has yet to persuade or compel the autonomous regions—especially those troublesome Andalucían socialists—to cut spending sufficiently.

For its part, the EU, France and Germany in particular, watch this situation unfold with terror in their hearts, as they do with all the PIIGS—especially Greece, where an even more severe variation on this theme is developing. The fear is due primarily to the fact that if

Spain and the rest implode, they will drag the euro—the same standard of value upon whose stability and sanctity Germany and France depend—down with them. If Spain goes into default and cannot cover its debts to other states and financial institutions, which it obviously cannot do without help, then its commitment to the neoliberal package will be irreparably violated. It will be impossible to contain domestic inflation, deficit, and debt levels, let alone long-term interest rates, which are hard to control at the best of times. Its credit rating, which rating agencies have already knocked down a couple of notches, will plummet. Without the confidence of the bond markets, it will only be able to raise funds on money markets by offering extraordinary yields. Worse, it won't be able to raise adequate funds by any means. Renegotiating or "rolling over" existing loans—which the central government and Catalunya and all the other *comunidades* must do very soon—will be equally fraught. None of this is unimaginable: in late July 2012, Spain had to pay 7.75 percent on its "benchmark" 10–year debt issue, far higher than what many policy-makers and financiers consider the 7 percent threshold marking bailout time. To get an idea of how relatively high that is, the "spread" between Spanish yields and that of German bonds exceeded 500 "basis points" for most of 2012, and hit 650 in July, higher than at any point since the introduction of the euro. ("Basis point" is the finance term for $1/100^{th}$ of a percent; a 650 basis point spread means that the German state can borrow money at 6.5 percent less than the Spanish state.)

Barring a massive and at best only temporarily effective "rescue package," default would almost certainly spark a run on both Spanish banks and Spanish bonds, precipitating panic across the Eurozone, making it impossible for the southern members in particular to service their debts. This is almost as certain to lead to something like a run on the euro, which would accelerate as it spread across the currency union. No international currency trader will want to be holding euros if Spain or anyone else goes down—indeed, they are already starting to "short" the euro, just as they did Asian currencies in 1997–98.

Hence the endless string of bailout discussions and "fiscal compact" negotiations overseen by the "Troïka": the European Commission, the ECB and the IMF. Most of these are in fact between Spain (or another of the PIIGS) and Germany and France, who will have to foot most of the bill, at least in the short term. Which means they have to sell the arrangements to their own increasingly pissed-off electorates. Many French and Germans view themselves in a manner similar to that by which Catalans judge their own region's role in the subsidization of Spanish indolence. Their patience for what they see as ceaseless pandering to economies that are doomed to remain backward and corrupt appears to be wearing thin.[77] But in the eyes of the govern-

---

77 The fact that many Germans think they are the only ones carrying the weight does not mean German capital or the German state are uninterested in a "fiscal compact," or that such an arrangement is high on the PIIGS wish list. Because the fiscal compact would give Germany a great deal of control over domestic finances in the Eurozone, they and the ECB are its biggest fans, since it would essentially "complete" the EU's full neoliberalization. Only members of the fiscal compact—which entails a commitment to vicious austerity in public spending and brutal "corrections" if the rules are broken—will have access to a newly created European Stability Mechanism. Such

ments of the EU core, there is little choice. Either they somehow save Spain and the rest, or they give up on the euro—which, at least in late 2012, is an option they say they will never consider. Some may be starting to accept the exit of the worst offender, Greece, and preparing to deal with the damage. So far, however, except for recent stirrings in the financial press, no major player has publicly accepted a possible end to monetary union—the "Lazarus option," so called because it would mean resurrecting national currencies. Soon, however, things might change. Perhaps one of the PIIGS, under the leadership of a radical-left coalition like Greece's SYRIZA, might go it alone, break the rules and make a real "choice" where they were told there is none.[78] Alternatively—and probably just as likely—we may witness a fracture initiated by quasi-fascist conservative nationalists unwilling and unable to stem the economic tide.[79] We shall see.

For its part, the Spanish government and the country's most powerful capitalists desperately tried to avoid having to be bailed out, since that involves, among other things, acquiescing to the austerity conditions with which the Troïka is obsessed. Yet they were (and still are) stuck with the same problem that

an agreement was in fact signed in March 2012, to come into effect 1 January 2013.

78 Slavoj Žižek, "Save Us from the Saviours," *London Review of Books*, volume 34, no. 11 (7 June 2012).

79 For example, the electoral platform of the Dutch far-right populist Geert Wilders includes closing the Netherlands' borders to immigration, exiting the currency union, and seceding from the EU; see "Dutch Rightwinger Turns Fire on Euro," *Financial Times* (27 August 2012).

has plagued capitalism increasingly frequently over the last decades—insolvent banks "too big to fail." The worst of these is Bankia, which is actually a product of the state's effort to save seven regional *cajas* or retail savings and loan banks. The *cajas*—whose board members, unsurprisingly, were closely connected to the Partido Popular (PP), Spain's ruling party—had, just as unsurprisingly, over-leveraged and over-loaned in the Spanish property bubble.[80] In 2010, they were salvaged with €4.5 billion of Spanish state funds and amalgamated into one large and unwieldy institution, Bankia, in an attempt to stave off depositors' and Spanish bond-holders' fears. It was not enough. By late Spring 2012, Madrid determined that an additional €19 billion was necessary, but that was money it just did not

---

80 As pointed out in the *Financial Times* (30 May 2012) the collapse of the *cajas* is basically a repeat of the US savings and loan crisis of the 1980s, and a product of the same gambling with depositors' money. This gamble seems like a good idea, because in the supposedly "normal" conditions of capitalism, short-term interest rates are lower than long-term interest rates, since the uncertainty associated with a loan increases the farther into the future the contract extends. If you graph it, the interest rate rises slowly as the term of the loan increases in duration. This is called the "yield curve" or the "term structure" of interest rates. Like the savings and loan banks in the US, the Spanish *cajas* bet on the stability of this relationship, and borrowed short-term money they then used to back longer-term loans (mostly mortgages and other retail products). As long as they were earning higher interest on the money loaned than they were paying on the money borrowed, it worked. But when the market went through turmoil, and the short term looked riskier than the long term, the yield curve "inverted," and they had to service debt at a higher interest rate than they were earning on their own loans. This situation could not last long, and in both cases it all fell apart.

have. The Bank of Spain, the relic of the nation's central bank, came up with a "radical" plan to make the funds available—"radical" being, again, a relative term: the idea was to give Bankia the money in the form of Spanish sovereign bonds, which it could then use as collateral to borrow from the ECB—but that only drove Spanish bond yields higher and infuriated the ECB and Germany.[81]

Still, Spain insisted it could figure everything out. But that certainly did not stop it from suggesting other means by which help could arrive and enable it to solve the problems more quickly, if only the ECB and Germany would listen to reason. For example, the European Financial Stability Fund (EFSF), which is intended to help national governments, could make an exception to the rules and make capital available to a bank. Or, even better, the ECB could underwrite (i.e., guarantee) Spanish sovereign debt. Most "radical" of all, however, is the idea that the EU would underwrite its member states' sovereign debt, via so-called "eurobonds," to relieve the pressure on issuer's finances. This of course would mean that Germany and the rest of the EU core would have to collectively back Spanish or Portuguese or Italian debt.

---

81 As a slightly "technical" side note, soaring Spanish sovereign bond yields are problematic not only because they raise borrowing costs for the Spanish state. They are also a grave concern because sovereign bonds are the form in which many domestic banks hold their capital reserves, and they serve as collateral for those banks on the interbank loan market. When the state that issued them looks shaky, it also means that it is much more difficult for Spanish banks to raise capital, which is of course what they desperately need to do.

Initially, the ECB and Germany rejected these suggestions. The monetary union was never supposed to lead to this. Without the capacity to tightly control Spanish state spending—which, unlike these "alternatives," a bailout would give them—these proposals lay dead in the water.[82] The chaos of the summer of 2012, however, meant that even these articles of faith had to be abandoned. With Spain's finances in tatters, Greece proving totally "untamable" (even though the centre-right squeaked by in the June election), and Italy teetering under an unelected technocracy, the Eurozone powers-that-be agreed to milder terms on Spain's €60 billion "rescue package," non-state loans from the EFSF, and, eventually and almost unbelievably, to the "nuclear deterrent"—effectively backing sovereign debt by promising to protect the euro come hell or high water.

All of this has fanned the flames of an Inquisition-like commitment to "austerity," the neo- and classical liberal cure-all, which burns at the core of European power. Sitting in judgment over the heretics in Spain, Greece, and the rest, northern European capital and their friends in government (this includes the British too, who, while not members of the Eurozone, are still thoroughly enmeshed in Europe) demand "austerity" throughout the EU, particularly in the PIIGS. Under German leadership, personified in Chancellor Angela

---

82 One of the few entertaining moments in the Eurozone crisis followed Spain's "acceptance" of its first chunk of rescue funds. Mariano Rajoy, Spanish president and increasingly *un*popular leader of the ironically named Partido Popular, returned home boasting of how tough he was, how he had made the powers-that-be back down and give him what Spain wanted. His ridiculous triumphant speech to the nation, and the subsequent rage on Angela Merkel's face, made for good comedy.

Merkel, they stipulate fidelity to neoliberal doctrine as the condition for any "bailouts" or "rescues" they might be able to coordinate via a range—some new, some long established—of nonetheless inadequate tools. These include, for example, the newly created European Stability Mechanism (ESM; the permanent replacement for the temporary EFSF), or the ECB, the IMF, additional loans from arm-twisted core-country banks, or negotiated sub-market yields on the redemption of outstanding bonds ("haircuts").[83]

But as any Keynesian will tell you, the glaring problem for capitalism is that austerity means abandoning these nation-states at precisely the moment their capitals need help the most. Indeed, it means stopping doing what little is being done. The idea behind austerity—and it is a very old one, at least two centuries old—is the same one resurrected by Reagan and Volcker in the crackdown on inflation a few decades ago: brutal pain in the supposed short term, in the interests of long-term recovery and growth. Never mind that "recovery" is likely to leave many behind, just as the Reagan-Volcker "recovery" set workers and the unemployed so far back they have never recovered (that was part of the point). As even the most self-interested and rabidly neoliberal bond traders are starting to realize, there is absolutely no guarantee that the pain of austerity will be short-term, or that its promise of a return to profitability and growth will be realized on any reason-

---

83 All of which—no surprise—are monetary, not fiscal, fixes. Economic orthodoxy can hardly even say the word "fiscal," as in "fiscal policy," like taxation or social welfare spending, without a sneer (unless, of course, they are talking about reducing them!).

able timeline, if at all. And it is worth pointing out that these concerns are lurking in the minds of people who couldn't give a damn about the poor. They are only interested in Spain's macro-conditions, which as we know are determined almost entirely by the relative influence of capital, the rich, the middle classes, and big industry and finance in particular.

The "radical" notion that austerity might not work has gained some purchase with Europe's political and economic elites as its failures in post-crisis Britain and France have become impossible to ignore. Perhaps the power of those chanting the mantra of austerity, at least in this historical variation, has started to loosen. François Hollande, the nominally "left" French president whose 2012 election ousted Merkel's sidekick Nicolas Sarkozy, aims to reanimate an "activist" growth plan for Europe, with US endorsement.[84] In Spain, and across southern Europe, the new talk of *crecimiento* (Spanish for "growth"), is welcome, if much belated, since the constant flight of capital from Spanish bonds and banks never slowed for all the months of austerity talk; on the contrary, it accelerated. Even the bond markets know austerity cannot work—which is not good news for capitalist nation-states, because now everyone knows it is possible *nothing* will work.

---

84 "Activism" describes the embrace of the state's capacity to provide market "stimulus," especially via monetary tools, and is as such vociferously denounced by advocates of austerity like former chair of the US Federal Reserve Alan Greenspan—see his diatribe "Activism" in the journal *International Finance*, volume 14, number 1 (Spring 2011), 165–82. It is available free online at http://www.cfr.org/content/publications/attachments/infi_1277_Rev6.pdf.

The most important question, for anticapitalists and for those interested in anything we might reasonably call well-being or social justice, is whether, and on what time scale, any of this panic-induced capitalist therapy will make any real difference at all. Bailout or default? Collapse now or collapse later? Certainly German capital and its allies have not given up on the austerity fix, and the vindictive "coalition" government in the UK remains obsessed with state retrenchment and privatization, despite being forced by its own electorate to change its tune somewhat in light of the social disaster its program has precipitated for everyone but the rich.

Moreover, those in Spain who take up the task of trying to deal with the repercussions of the crisis are not necessarily less committed to neoliberalism. For these include not only the activists and others on the ground struggling to weather the storm and prepare for the next one, but also Spain's liberal and illiberal politicians and financiers, its landed elites and industrialists—those who kowtow daily to northern masters. Their main contribution to the debate is not to say that the rules that demand austerity are flawed, but that "actually" Spain is in much better shape than the ECB, France, and Germany believe. Yet they face the additional challenge of working with what they must see as the perverse ass-end of neoliberal political economy. Their task, more complex than any being undertaken in Berlin, is to figure out how to please the bosses in the world's financial centres by further squeezing a mutinous, disrespectful, and regionally- and class-fragmented population—the most vocal segment of which has been dubbed *los indignados*—much of which is unwilling to accept the fundamental postulate of capitalist governance: privatize the gains, socialize the losses.

This is only possible if the state can do its job as the "factor of cohesion," if it can be effectively mobilized in the practice of hegemony. In Spain, this is increasingly difficult, and may turn out to be as impossible as in Greece. For the poor, the pre-crisis boom hardly did any good at all, and for most of the rest, its legacy is mainly one of dashed hopes. The Spanish state's role in the hegemony of capital is clearly more and more peripheral—a problem that the currency union unwittingly did more to bring about than any other force. Now it tells the country's workers they must endure decades of relative penury to pay for the absurd indiscretions of bankers who have probably fled to their second or third homes in London, Berlin, or Geneva, if they were not from there already. In poor, traditional strongholds of socialism like Andalucía, those workers no longer understand the state as a "factor of cohesion," and they are consequently increasingly willing to give *un corte de mangas* to the political and economic powers-that-be.[85] It is not that they are so naïve as to believe they have discovered a radical path to prosperity; what they know is that the tumult is coming no matter how compliant they are.

In response, the liberals and conservatives in Madrid stamp their feet and swear, *absolutely correctly* in light of neoliberal logic, that if the Spanish people are unwilling to pay the costs then no one will, and the ship is going down with all hands. If Spain wants to play by

---

85 *Hacer un corte de mangas* ("to cut the sleeves") is the Spanish term for that distinctive "fuck you" gesture in which the bent arm is thrust upward while the other hand grips the biceps.

the rules, or if they want even to stay within view of the rules, it is true: there is no choice.

However conspiratorial or self-interested one might imagine their motives, Spanish leadership, whoever that is or will be in the future, and however democratically representative, is unquestionably eager to "save" the Spanish economy. In the current context, and playing by existing rules, there appears to be only one way to do that. This is why many of the regional socialist parties, like the Partit dels Socialistes de Catalunya, more or less endorse Madrid's austerity plan. My point is not that you can't even trust socialists any more, which may or may not be true. My point, rather, is that there is no need to unmask evil or greed at the heart of the Spanish state to explain its attempt to contort the nation into a fiscal position that makes the ECB, Germany, or the bond markets happy. When socialists give up socialism to placate capital (or give up bothering to pretend they hadn't abandoned it long ago), as they have in Catalunya and all over the world since the end of the Long Boom, it is unacceptable to attribute it simply to political cowardice or self-interested ideological disarmament.[86]

On the contrary, the explanation is far more straightforward: capital won. Sometimes with armies, sometimes with persuasion, sometimes with money, and sometimes by accident, but it won. For at least the last thirty or forty years, and this is increasingly true in nom-

---

86 Think, for example, of Lula da Silva, metalworker and long-time union activist, who became Brazil's President (2003–2010) and presided over the nation's rise as one of the principle players in neoliberal global political economy. Any explanation of Lula's abandonment of socialism must go far beyond simple moralizing or macho activist hectoring.

inally "noncapitalist" nation-states like China also, capital has proven richer, more powerful, more expansive, more convincing, and more *real* than any other political economic force on the planet. It is not a myth, it is not an elaborate hoax, and its wealth and dominance are not fictitious or illusory. Unsurprisingly, therefore, it has written the political economic rule book by which the world plays, *and* defined the terms and means by which one might "legitimately" break those rules. Socialists may have lost their ideological fire, or they may have proven weak-kneed, but there is good reason for it. They read the writing on the wall and decided that given the options available to them, and the ultimate political and economic objectives to which socialism aims, i.e., the long-term betterment of citizens' everyday lives, their constituencies had to play by the rules, and the rules rule against being socialists.

To return, then, to the question of whether the decisions taken to stave off (or not) the collapse of the euro will ultimately have any significance at all for a nation like Spain, what the socialists confront is a conceptual and material frame of reference provided by capitalism alone, i.e., the overwhelmingly hegemonic *reality* of capitalism. What they recognize is that to reject its dictates would probably make a huge difference—but not a "good" difference. For it means taking risks they, at least, were unwilling to take, because to dismiss the existing order seems to them very likely to mean plunging into no order at all. Where, Spanish socialists ask themselves, is Spain to go if it does not act out the neoliberal performance? What will it be? Who will it support? Certainly it seems more than reasonable to assume that the poor will not be better served by an isolated, stagnant and fragmented social fabric. If so, rejecting capital will hardly appear more effective in meeting their immediate needs.

Now, I am no anthropologist, but my conversations, my reading of the newspapers, and my general sense is that while many Spaniards are categorically against the *recortes*, the cuts in state spending austeritites demand, they feel they have few if any alternatives. They oppose Madrid's obedient destruction of the social safety net, but they also see it as inevitable. This very real, and completely understandable, political resignation is in fact a larger-scale version of the wage-worker's bind, and it is equally crucial for anticapitalists to take it seriously and to try to understand. Indeed, however "radical" we might imagine our politics, we must recognize ourselves in it. If we cannot see in it the actual material and social constraints experienced by real living individuals and groups in their everyday attempts to make and remake a way to be in the world, then we will never find a way out of it. If we cannot understand that capitalism, and the agency of the billions of people who have little "choice" but to embrace it, is a product of far more than the trickery and ill-will of a few, an effective mass-based anticapitalist politics is to my mind a pipe-dream.

WHAT SORT OF PATHS TO WHAT SORT OF FUTURE?

On 24 May 2012, *El País*, the main "left" daily in Spain, ran an article entitled "A change of course at last? The threat of a broken euro illuminates an alternative to austerity." The "alternative," however, is not all that alternative: *financiación y liquidez*, ECB-backed financing and liquidity for "growth." This is a perfect example of the ways in which neoliberal capital determines even the ways in which its rules can be broken, and it exposes to plain view the range of "choices" circulating in policy circles.

If I have done the job that I hoped to do with this book, this alternative that is not an alternative will be entirely unsurprising. Not because of capitalism's lack of imagination, or its conservatism or greed and so forth, but because of its systemic imperatives, its material and ideological binds, its logic and incentives, its "overdetermination" of things "economic" in much of the world. Despite its current lack of fashion on the left, I cannot think of a better term for this mode of power than "structural." Capitalism so saturates everyday life, particularly in the global North, that even many who actively oppose its power reproduce its hegemony in many of the acts necessary for merely being in the world. It determines the ways and means through which we live, and consequently, we live it into being. This is not to suggest in any way, however, that all that is required to overturn it, therefore, is a simple act of will. There is a long history of left critique of "voluntarism"—the idea that to change the world all we have to do is decide what the world should look like and just go make it so—that, while it often seems like a wet blanket, needs to be taken seriously.

Of course the will to change will be a key component of the tools for change, but there are also structural, historical, and contingent forces at work that militate against a naïve plan to "build a dream" that does not emerge from and build upon the world in which we live. We cannot start with an idealized Utopia at the end of history and work backward to figure out how we get there. History is filled with evidence of the failures of utopianism, whether it takes the macro-form of the Bolshevik revolution, or the micro-form of escapist "intentional communities." Marx and Engels' critique of utopian socialists, those who believe history can be readily broken or dismissed, still stands. We must begin from where we are.[87]

I am aware that the overwhelming tenor of this book—in its account of capitalist wealth and ideological power, in its analysis of capitalism's unprecedented robustness and capacity for technical and institutional innovation, and so forth—might seem more than a little pessimistic. If the analysis and history is right, then an anticapitalism that is interested in a better world has a daunting task ahead, one that will prove incredibly difficult if it is possible at all. But that seems to me the truth of the matter. It will be difficult, and it may be impossible, and I think it essential we face up to this, and not try to convince ourselves that the key can be found in subversive play, or love, or community, or imagination. These may all be essential, but there is no magical but as-yet untrodden path over, under, or around the grim reality of capitalism. One of the consistent failures of utopianism lies in the belief that it is really just a straightforward act of creation or will to envision a new world, that the main questions about that new world can be answered before we get there, and that once we have shed the ways of this (capitalist) world, the route to the new one will readily appear. It may sound depressing, but it is not so. We must find our way out, and we must start from the densely entangled core. We will only be able to figure out our route, or routes, as we go.

Still, however pessimistic or depressing, I categorically refuse the idea that this stance is defeatist. That these routes will be difficult, and that they may never

---

87 See Chapter III of the *Manifesto*.

lead to a noncapitalist "real freedom," in no way means that therefore things are hopeless, or that it is not worth trying. Nor does it mean that escaping or overcoming capitalism *per se* is impossible. On the contrary, that, at least, appears to me not only possible but inevitable. But anticapitalism, despite its rather vague "negative" self-description, obviously cannot be simply anticapitalist. It cannot stop at "ABC," anything-but-capitalism. Even a brief glance at the past suggests there are several noncapitalist ways of organizing the world that make capitalism look pretty good in comparison—the slave-plantation mode, the authoritarian state socialist mode, and so forth. If all we want is noncapitalism, then it seems to me the surest way to get there is to leave it to the capitalists—the terrible knowledge of this truth is in fact the fundamental premise of Keynesianism. In the current context, a complete embrace of laissez-faire is, if nothing else, certain to bring about catastrophic climate change and ecological decay, and like any other historical mode of production, capitalism cannot outlive its resource base for long. The most brutally effective anticapitalist strategy right now would be to applaud and spur on the terrifying atmospheric and environmental acts of violence in which capital is now enthusiastically engaged.

However, for what I hope are obvious social justice reasons—reasons, it is worth emphasizing, that are not necessarily radical—I think that strategy would be disastrous. Capitalism may be undone this way, but the costs will be borne disproportionately by those who benefit least from the existing system. The only secure communities, if any, are likely to be those militarized ecological havens for the once-capitalist rich predicted by compelling doom-sayers like Mike Davis.[88] Our task is not merely to undo capitalism, but to achieve something better. Unfortunately, if climate science is correct, we do not have much time to pull this off, and we will not be able to choose the contexts in which we work. Capital may be "victorious," in an ecologically limited way, for quite a while. Or we may soon see the end of its reign. Either eventuality will demand that we do our utmost to ensure that the end of capitalism prepares the ground for something better—freer, more secure, more just, less violent and arbitrary. Those efforts will entail a great deal of experimentation and failure. The answers are not obvious, and no matter how logically or strategically sound anticapitalist analysis is, no matter how well it can anticipate and organize, it can neither guarantee success nor prevent failure.

The struggle is ultimately over the future as such, and more precisely for a politically adequate but open range of futures, not over competing "correct" visions of what we can become and how to achieve it. If we can indeed get to "better places," whatever they are, they will entail a differentiated collection of noncapitalisms, their forms shaped substantially by changing and geographically disparate political economic and social conjunctures along the way. Moreover, the (at least) short-term persistence of capitalism is certain to be among the principal forces producing such conjunctures. Ecological limits, popular resentment, and political instability make a sociopolitically chaotic, but nominally capitalist, mode of production highly likely in the next decades. So, rather than imagine the future as all or nothing, ei-

---

88 "Who Will Build the Ark?," *New Left Review*, series II, no. 61 (January–February 2010), 29–46.

ther the victory of "progressive" anticapitalist forces, or the complete apocalyptic defeat of anticapitalist efforts, we should take as par for the course the failures, unintended consequences, and successes (great and small) that are sure to come in the years ahead.

We also need to reflect on the possibilities available, given the range of potential changes we may actually be able to organize. If we can render capitalism terminally ill, the ecological and social crises it bequeaths us will not pause while we figure out what to do. This is among the most pressing challenges for any emerging political economic alternative. Capitalism is likely to leave us with a catastrophe, but its culpability will not provide cover; an ineffective anticapitalist response will move no one. The world will likely be falling apart. Noncapitalist modes of production will not have time to methodically "figure things out." So the problem is not only to identify capitalism's limits, blind spots, and flaws, but also to understand where its failures are leading us, and what we might need to do to achieve something meaningful in the world capitalism is constructing, but won't survive long enough to see.

To close this final chapter, then, it might be helpful to return to some of the elements of capitalism analyzed in Part I, to consider at a necessarily broad scale what might become of them. What of money and the state in a noncapitalist world? What of markets and firms in a noncapitalist mode of production? What choices are we given, or, if not given, might we take? I feel great trepidation tackling these questions, and not only because it is self-important to suggest that I have answers. Many men and women, with much more experience and wisdom than me, have written on the same questions.

Where my contribution is not merely speculative, it is bound to be derivative of people you would be better served to read or listen to or speak to yourself. Yet it seems just as ridiculous, even irresponsible, not to suggest some brief and limited conclusions.

In my "scholarly" writing, I have struggled for years with the problem of money in capitalism. For a long time I was convinced that we could never get beyond capitalism without getting rid of money, even though, as I argued in Chapter 3, you can have money without capitalism. Ultimately, I believed, money is the absolutely essential foundation for capitalism, especially contemporary capitalism. While it may be possible or even likely that in a post-capitalist world something like money might reappear, I was sure we needed to destroy it to get there. The problem seemed to me to lie in the fact that capitalist money, as a social relation or institution, militated against all meaningful political change. Because it must carry and stabilize value across time and space, and because all or virtually all exchange takes place via money, money is at root a promise that the future, here or elsewhere, will be basically the same as today. If it were not, no one would trust money as the expression of value, and then it would not be money. So ending the rule of money and value seemed to me an essential precondition for a world other than the one we have.

Most anticapitalists to whom I made this argument over the years were willing to grant me its basic logic, but nonetheless looked at me like I was little crazy. For many, getting rid of money seems even less likely than getting rid of capitalism. In many ways, it seems that way to me too. Moreover, it is not at all obvious how we might do so. In 1919, Keynes famously quoted Lenin as having said that "the best way to destroy the Capitalist System is to debauch the currency."[89] As far as I know Lenin never said this, but whether he did or not, it is not true. To "debauch the currency" is not equivalent to eliminating money. Capitalist and noncapitalist currencies have been debauched many times, and although it has certainly caused the societies in question great pain each time, capitalism has in fact proven itself the quickest of all modes of production to recover from the debauching, usually even stronger, at least from a monetary perspective.

The inimitable Japanese anarchist Kojin Karatani, reading Marx and pondering these and many other questions, has come to what might seem the rather mystical conclusion that "money should exist, money should not exist."[90] Karatani suggests this condition—which he calls an "antinomy," a term that the eighteenth-century philosopher Immanuel Kant used to describe a contradiction that is by definition unresolvable—is part of the many inevitably undecidable features of anticapitalist struggle. In other words, there is no correct answer to the question "what should we do about money?" While he does not go into those capital-guaranteeing features of money that trouble me so much, I feel confident he would concur. But at the same time, money, if not capitalist money, is an essential means of exchange between different individuals and different communities, and Karatani is committed to the idea that it is only in exchange (not capitalist exchange), in the in-between

---

89 *Economic Consequences of the Peace*, http://www.gutenberg. org/ebooks/15776, chapter VI, paragraph 13.

90 *Transcritique: On Kant and Marx* (Cambridge: M.I.T. Press, 2003), 22.

spaces where sociality happens and people can interact, that something like a noncapitalist, nonstate future can unfold. So we must have it, and must not have it, at the same time. Consequently, Karatani finds hope in so-called "local exchange trading systems," or LETS—local moneys that circulate in, and are intended for use by, local communities.

There is a lot in Karatani's ideas I find compelling. But, like most of us, I struggle with how to come to grips with antinomy in my political life. I am, however, convinced that there are many questions we must ask of ourselves, our communities and our world for which there is no correct answer. I would even venture to suggest that the more important the question, the more likely this is the case. Facing that fact, and the political "fear and trembling" it precipitates, seems to me a necessary existential variation on the need to analyze capitalism with "sober realism."

With regard to money, then, I believe that one way to act in the shadow of inevitable contradiction and uncertainty is to actively demonetize realms of social life we can make better without money. I do not mean "demonetize" as it is used in the business media, where the term refers to capital converting assets from money to nonmoney value-forms. Nor do I mean producing our own moneys, like LETS or bitcoin, a nonstate, digital currency recently developed for "P2P" (person to person) internet-based exchange. These might be very useful tools in anticapitalist efforts, certainly, but they are still moneys, and reproduce some if not all of the barriers to change identified above. I don't even mean to argue for barter exchange-systems, which are also a powerful way of escaping the constant surveillance by the state and capital that modern money makes possible, especially in its electronic forms.

Instead, by "demonetize" I mean to provide what we can to others, to the extent that we are able, for free. In part, this would be to demonetize the exchange of what we have to offer in our capacity as waged or un-waged workers—so that I, for example, might teach a course or write an article for free. But even further, and more importantly, I mean something closer to what I see everyday in the life of people like my friends Matt and Selena, who come closer than anyone I know to con-fronting capitalism with both sober realism and a refusal to play by the rules.[91] They live according to a principle I have heard others call "radical generosity": they share virtually all that they have, including their home, their meals, their time, and their intellects, with those who otherwise have no access to those resources. They do not expect payment, exchange, or applause. They just do it. And when they need help, they ask for it, with-out a lot of sorry-to-bother-yous and I-wouldn't-other-wise-asks—which are unnecessary anyway, at least with most of the people they are asking. Of course, they have to pay for food and cover their children's needs and they like to have a glass of wine or a beer sometimes. They both work for wages often, taking payment from their employers in return for their labour. But there is no idle surplus in their home, whatever comes in is available to

---

91 They are equally impressive people, but for those not in Van-couver BC, Matt (whose last name is Hern) is more accessible than Selena, since he has written and edited several excellent books, including *Field Day: Getting Society out of School* (Van-couver: New Star, 2003), *Everywhere, All the Time* (Oakland: AK, 2008), and *Common Ground in a Liquid City: Essays in Defense of an Urban Future* (Oakland: AK, 2010).

the people in their community, and scores, even hundreds, of people have gained from it over the years, myself and my family included. Moreover, unsurprisingly, many of those people have returned the gesture, creating a sort of ephemeral, low-carbon, no-money zone, at least in some significant segments of everyday life, like eating and sleeping and reading, that are for most people highly carbon-intensive and money/income-dependent.

This way of living is a fundamental, if micro-scale, challenge to the rule of value in capitalism and the kinds of competitive, accumulation-oriented social relationships it endorses. It challenges the power of price by rejecting the logic of equivalence upon which exchange is supposed to be predicated. It thus challenges the hegemony of markets and their constituent firms too, if to a limited degree, since a lot of what is shared, at least materially, is accessed on those markets from those firms. But as much or more valuable than anything else is that the whole set of relationships this approach to life sustains reminds everyone involved that they are not alone, that they are facing a daunting future enmeshed in a web of mutual support.

While in some ways a "small gesture," embedded as it is in a larger capitalist context, it is certainly tempting to say something like "Imagine what it would be like if we all—or if everyone who had the resources—lived like that. We could change the world." Despite my own knee-jerk reaction to all things rose-coloured, I must admit we might well. The difficulty, however, lies not in imagining (at least not in this case). The difficulty lies in doing more than just imagining if everyone lived like this, and in figuring out how to make it so. How do we carve out demonetized spaces large enough to stand as significant barriers to capital? The idea that we might "convince" (if that is the right term) "everyone" to live like this is naïve. If nothing else, there are far too many people spatially concentrated in communities and places without the resources to simply start to provide for each other. For billions of people—many of whom do in fact function in such networks far more than most people in the global North—it is hard enough just to get adequate food and shelter for the members of their family.

Many of those people already live for all intents and purposes outside the circulation of capital, and are desperate to find a way in. A livelihood has no special merit just because it is "noncapitalist," and compared to what they have, a life ruled by capital is certainly desirable to many who are "free" of its domination. There is a reason that Chinese dissidents flee to the US. If you are struggling to get by as a peasant and wage work looks comparatively attractive, or if you live in a community ruled by a "communist" police state, then the US, for all its massive problems, looks good, especially from afar. That basically nobody willingly immigrates from the capitalist to the noncapitalist parts of the world is not merely a function of ideology. The fact that in many cases it is the power of capital, via neocolonial imperialism or environmental destruction, that makes noncapitalist life so hard does nothing to diminish immediate need. It is one more reason to be anticapitalist, but we must recognize that for many in the global North (though not all), it is in fact relative privilege that provides the security to seek something beyond capitalism, and much of that security is provided by the power of capital.

This is in no way to say that "radical generosity" is not worthwhile. In the grand macro-scheme of things it is a small gesture, geographically and politically—although not for the people doing the giving, who sometimes live with a lot less flexibility, material comfort, and security than they would otherwise. But as it stands, the power of capital in the global North, and in particular the tenacious grip of its "bindings"—which include its relative merits in the eyes, for example, of young people in rural China or those who experienced Stalinist brutality—mean that small gestures are necessary, both initially and throughout the process of anticapitalist efforts. In the wealthy world at least, we cannot get where we need to go, wherever that is, in one "great leap forward." An anticapitalist social formation cannot be built out of the raw material of capitalism as it currently exists. We must recognize its power, and work to prepare a ground upon which greater and greater change is both materially and ideologically possible.

Some, like the indefatigable Slavoj Žižek, see immediate potential for a radical and socially just anticapitalism in the disintegration of the euro and the fall of the Torquemadas of neoliberal austerity, and especially in the rise of the radical left in Greece. They call for international solidarity with the Greek people in their rejection of the dictates of international finance capital and liberal ideology. I echo their calls, and share their hope. If Greece can eventually achieve something even close to what Žižek thinks possible, it will be a truly "historic" moment, in the most weighty sense of the word. But that moment looks less and less imminent, and even if it came to pass, Greece is not a part of the core of global capital, and "Grexit" (as financial insiders have nicknamed Greek exit from the euro) will not end the reign of capital. Call me glass-half-empty for saying so, but a wave of Greece-like breakaways is unlikely to diffuse across western Europe and North America. A coalition of the radical left like that led by SYRIZA is not on the immediate horizon in the centres of capitalist power. Indeed, even in these depths, SYRIZA appears to speak for less than half of Greece's voters, so it is important not to exaggerate the solidarity of the "Greek people." Moreover, Greece has decades of radical left anticapitalist activism and political life to draw upon, an admirable history of resistance to vicious military dictatorship, and a level of material deprivation among a substantial proportion of its citizens—historically, at least, the most effective argument against a mode of production—that the capitalist core has not experienced in living memory.

In that core, the part of the world with which I am most familiar, we need a different plan. We have more, and different, political work to do than Greek anticapitalists, and, for the moment, we lack the same level of material incentive to break the rules. I believe that plan must share at least one thing with Greece, however: it must focus in the short term on the state—which means that while it must be transnational, anticapitalism must also take particular forms in particular places, based on existing geographies of power. This is what Gramsci and Poulantzas, in their own ways, said too. At present, the state, within its territory and in its participation in multilateral institutions and contracts, is the essential means by which capital's hegemony is legitimized and protected. Consequently, it is the principal institutional means by which to influence the distribution of the material means for human well-being. At least in the near term, the state's legitimacy as the mechanism of distribution is axiomatic: it is the legitimate mechanism of distribution within its territory *because* it is the state. Via a suite of widely accepted domains of responsibility—taxes, fiscal spending, monetary governance, social programs, labour regulation, market oversight, etc.—the state is the distributional centre of gravity. If mass anticapitalist movements are to emerge in the global North, at least, then anticapitalists must work to gain control of this hegemonic distributional mechanism. If abject poverty and deprivation is unacceptable, which it surely is, then demonstrating that it need not exist is an essential goal, and the state seems to me crucial to the construction of a new hegemony based on this principle.

Moreover, the state at present represents the most effective means to environmental regulation, perhaps especially with regard to climate change. In the long run, I believe, that state will be a fetter to an ecologically just world, but current levels of carbon emission and biodiversity loss may rule out a human long run if we do not put the tools at hand to work immediately and effectively. Contrary to orthodox faith in market-driven innovation—which, if anything, is focused on burning up every last bit of carbon stored in the Earth's crust before regulations or catastrophe make it unprofitable— the state's regulatory and funding apparatus seems to me by far the most powerful such tool in the near term.

However, taking the reins of the state will be neither easy, nor quick, nor unproblematic. At the very least, the state has its own problems and historical legacy of injustice and hierarchy. If the state cannot stand sovereign above the people as an historical "exclusionary device" depriving some because they "do not belong," we must not only take the state—as the site of capital-P Politics—we must also engage the ordinary and extraordinary political realm. These efforts, which are already underway across the world, are by definition innumerable. They mark creative and usually geographically specific responses or challenges. Many of them do not explicitly engage the state *per se*, and many of them are not even necessarily explicitly anticapitalist: local food movements, resistance to resource extraction and destruction, squatters' rights work, "tax-fairness" efforts, antipoverty and antihunger movements; the list goes on. But most of these movements, through no fault or lack of imagination of their own, are embedded in an overwhelmingly capitalist matrix. They are islands in an ocean. More islands are always a welcome sight, but the ocean remains.

Overcoming capitalism will be a tough climb up the scree-slope of history, so this is in no way to dismiss these efforts. We will all be impoverished if they do not flourish, and it is hard to imagine they will not be an essential part of a noncapitalist world. The idea that no one will need to struggle for social justice after capitalism is gone seems pretty naïve. Nevertheless, I would suggest that an essential move in the attempt to gradually (but not *too* gradually) build a world in which noncapitalisms can blossom, is to demand from capital and its states and planetary institutions the stuff of life—adequate shelter, food, and water, and the love, fun and prosperity made possible by a confidence in the fact that these essentials will be there tomorrow and the day after, no matter one's individual fortune. That confidence is the only meaningful sense freedom can have, and to be free is to have that confidence. We must demand unceasingly, then, the stuff of life that makes it possible, not because it is impossible for capital to deliver and will break capitalism, but because it is there to be had, more than enough. I suppose it is possible, as I mentioned earlier (Chapter 4), that if capitalism met those demands, we would have reached the anticapitalist goal, since what remains might not be capitalism. But the point would be moot.

This, as I take it, is what Žižek means when he says that resistance to capital is "surrender."[92] Capitalism is far too robust and entrenched materially and ideologically to imagine we can battle it by something called "resistance." Resistance would suggest we have some noncapitalist haven in the middle of it all which we must liberate or keep free from capital's tentacles. But in much of the world, those spaces, if they indeed exist, are inadequate, materially or politically, to an enduring noncapitalist mode of life. To do that we must not only "resist," we must demand—in the streets, at the ballot box, in parliaments, in the foyers of the financial districts' skyscrapers, at police stations, and elsewhere. Moreover, we need not demand anticapitalism. That, as we know, comes in many forms we do not want. What we demand will be time and place specific, but it will almost certainly not be "freedom" or "rights," but the space and resources in which to enjoy them. Freedom without adequate food and water is not freedom, and abstract "liberty" is meaningless or impossible without the material stuff of life.

I believe the main reason to be anticapitalist is that capital deprives most of the world of precisely this stuff of life. Against all evidence, capitalist reason claims that capital's goal is to provide for everyone, and thus exhorts us to embrace it, to give it time to work things out—"no

---

92 Slavoj Žižek, "Resistance Is Surrender," *London Review of Books*, volume 29, number 22 (15 November 2007).

pain, no gain." Some, of course, hedge their bets, saying capitalism is "the best we can do," or the "least bad" way of organizing our political economic lives. That, it seems to me, is horseshit, and not a shred of evidence supports it. At my most generous, I might grant that capitalism, relative to what came before, is among the better ways developed thus far, but even setting aside the potentially suicidal nature of its relationship to its ecological bases, why would we ever accept something because it is the best "so far?" Imagine if we had stopped at leeching or slavery because they were the best methods for medicine and agriculture we had developed "so far."

The problem with capitalism is not that it makes us "unfree." Freedom and unfreedom are social categories, and their content has always been determined by the historical and geographical conditions in which they come to have meaning. We cannot "demand" freedom itself, as if it were a token or meal; neither the state nor capital, with all their riches, can give it to us, even if they wanted to. We can only demand, and if necessary take, the material and political means to a world in which freedom, whatever that comes to mean, can be exercised by all. The most fundamental problem with capitalism, and the reason it must be rejected, is that it is *structured*, in its very operation, to make it impossible for millions and even billions to be free in any meaningful sense. The critique of capitalism has little to do with how well it provides for the people of the world relative to what came before (feudalism, slave-plantations, etc.), or with a need to defend the disastrous attempts to resist it (Stalinist "communism," faux-socialist kleptocracy, etc.). Anticapitalism has to do, rather, with the fact that capitalism is not good enough. It is unacceptable.

What a detailed knowledge of capitalism can do, then, is help us see that despite what common wisdom suggests, capital's rules are not history's or nature's rules. If they are capital's rules, then anticapitalism need not respect them. It can also help us understand how what we have now might or might not be part of the innumerable experimental attempts necessary to get to the places we must go. There are, for example, compelling socialist critics like Benjamin Kunkel and Robin Blackburn who believe that a socialized but equally sophisticated financial system will be an essential element of any socialism to come, and their vision is based in a thorough and detailed understanding of the existing financial system and the ways in which it can and cannot be reworked.[93]

I used to believe I knew the future of finance in a just world—that there could be no such thing—but I am no longer so sure.[94] Either way, the core task of all the experiments to come, and the visions that sustain them, will be to demonstrate, by demanding it, that they can produce and sustain worlds in which the stuff of life is there for everyone and denied to none. If there is a way to do that, freedom will take care of itself. This, I would argue, is an eminently non-utopian ideal. The point is not to escape, to start over, to make an "imaginative leap"; not to discover the revolutionary X latent in all of us, or to "remake humanity" (as the most

---

93 Benjamin Kunkel, "Forgive Us Our Debts," *London Review of Books*, volume 34, number 9 (10 May 2012); Robin Blackburn, "The Subprime Crisis," *New Left Review*, series II, number 50 (2008), 63–106; and "Crisis 2.0," *New Left Review* series II, number 72 (2011), 33–62.

94 Geoff Mann, "Colletti on the Credit Crunch," *New Left Review*, series II, number 56 (2009), 119–27.

chilling of "communist" theoreticians often put it). The point is to keep developing ways to allow everyone to live unafraid of others or what the future might bring.

To be honest, it does not matter to me how we pull this off. I have what I consider compelling evidence for a materialist account of the ways change can and cannot happen, but there can be no monopoly on a truth not yet realized. We will not stumble upon one best strategy or idea. The ideas and politics will likely be multiple, and will continue to multiply. I imagine that the eclectic mix of failures, successes, and unintended outcomes this will produce will include both the radical generosity of Matt and Selena and more "traditional" struggles over state power, resources, and distribution. The power of this concatenation cannot help but change the grounds upon which subsequent struggles unfold, which is cru-cial, because we are in for a long fight. The exit is there, but we can't see it from where we are sitting.

The potential collapse of the euro, or the capitalist infrastructure, institutions, and logic that sustain it, has led to a collection of prognostications from observers all over the world. They cover the gamut, but they tend to either end of a spectrum. Before the Greek election in June 2012, SYRIZA and its supporters circulated a set of proposals under the heading "the exit from the crisis is on the left." These include a suite of rather "predict-able" but exciting and welcome demands: income redis-tribution, taxation of the rich, an extensive social safety net, debt cancellation, a reconfiguration of European governance, independent foreign policy, environmental regulation and restoration, and more. The underlying message is that SYRIZA, if it takes state power, will agree to stay in the EU only if its demands are met. While the proposals do not say how all this will be accomplished, beyond a manifesto-like "it will be so," the general tone resonates for many on the radical left. The old system is history, or soon will be. Its rejection is the future, and a radical future at that. This future will win out if we demand it. As SYRIZA puts it, "The incumbent economic and social system has failed, and we must overthrow it! … We are changing the future; we are pushing them into the past."

The other end of the spectrum is much less optimistic. It appeared in one of its more eloquent and compelling forms in *El País* on 1 June 2012, in a long opinion piece written by three orthodox Spanish economists working at elite universities in the US and the UK.[95] They argue that the Spanish government must be far more committed to the EU and the euro, and that it must reject Greek-style populist power-plays. No country, they say, has benefitted more than Spain from the ECB's liquidity injections during the crisis, and wherever the blame for the crisis ultimately falls, no one is presently tackling the political obstacles to dealing with it. Without the help of the EU and the ECB, they say, default and euro exit are highly likely. And, in marked contrast to SYRIZA's bold embrace of the future, they say that however bad many expect the "exit" scenario to be, it is likely to be far worse. Those "enchanted by the siren's song" that promises an escape from public and private debt don't realize that "the day after the exit, the situation is going to get very complicated": the new cur-

---

95 Jesus Fernandez-Villaverde, Luis Garicano, and Tano Santos, "No queremos volver a la España de los 50" ["We do not want to go back to the Spain of the 1950s"], *El País* 1 de junio de 2012, 33.

rency will be worth substantially less, wages and pensions will lose much of their value, import prices will rise. Businesses will go bankrupt, as will the public sector and banks. Global trade relations will fall apart, as firms are unable to play their part in supply chains. "Then," they write, "to give the new money credibility, and to avoid hyperinflation in the midst of falling incomes, the state will try to undertake a brutal fiscal consolidation, eliminating the deficit all at once, the same thing we are refusing to do right now."

The problem, they say, is not that the outcome will be the same either way, so we might as well do it now. The problem is that when—as orthodoxy always assumes—everything is cleared up, however many years or decades down the road, the Spain that re-emerges will not be today's Spain, but Spain of the 1950s, "low-cost, low-income, low-productivity, tourism-dependent, and with control brutally exercised by local *caciques* who will run the monopolies of the new closed economy…. A new privileged class with a firm grip on power, well-adapted for corruption, swindling and nepotism."

There are several damning critiques one might aim at this forecast. It assumes the persistence of current structural imperatives in the "new" Spain, and thus takes "austerity" as an inevitable result of "living beyond our means." It assumes the permanence of capitalist hegemony and a political culture that is merely an "isolated" version of what now exists, as if capitalist relations of production and distribution are a product of nature, and so on. I do not recommend taking the forecast seriously on its analytical grounds, which are as unimaginative and arrogantly blinkered as most of orthodoxy. Rather, despite its logical flaws, its predictable categories and causal mechanisms—despite the fact that it is in so many ways *wrong*, logically, ethically, and politically— we must take it seriously because it is nonetheless very likely true. At this conjuncture in the history of capitalism, in Europe and throughout the global North, their vision of the future is not at all far from Spain's future if it leaves the Eurozone. *Franquismo* without Franco is a very real possibility.

I know much less about Greece, and cannot predict where Greece might land in the event that SYRIZA or some other group leads it out of the Eurozone. I applaud them and support them and hope with all my heart that it works out as they plan, but assuming they can indeed win control of state institutions, I have little sense of where they will go, or how they will get there. I would like to believe that in five years we might look at Greece, or the people who live where Greece now is, and see it and them as a model, as proof. Yet, although I almost feel guilty saying it, I do not anticipate being able to do that. Perhaps because five years is not enough time, and it will take longer, or perhaps because it has already fallen apart, or half-fallen apart. I do not know.

Nonetheless, even though the political economist in me anticipates failure, the anticapitalist in me sees success in that failure (if it unfortunately comes to pass), regardless of how total it is. For the difference between Greece and Spain right now, or the difference between the Greek and Spanish political possibilities right now, is that some anticapitalists in Greece, and clearly a not-insignificant portion of the Greek electorate, are ready and willing to break the rules, to experiment boldly, to try, and even to fail. This seems to me the greatest and most valuable anticapitalist quality right now: a willingness and energy to refuse the structural bind of capitalism, to boldly fail, in imagination, analysis, logic, organization, strategy.[96] This requires extraordinary courage, and it is easy to forget that courage generally comes from either having nothing to lose, or from having no real fear of losing. It is the many people in between, who fear losing what little stability and hope capitalism currently provides, or who believe that capital might yet deliver on its promises, that acquiesce or embrace the rules. Anticapitalists' greatest political task, along with the experiments ongoing and to come, is to reach these folks, to help make sense of their experience in a way that does not belittle their hesitation. These are the people who feel their whole world is on the line; they have good reason for being reluctant to exchange it for what often sounds like empty promises, or worse.

All this requires an inexhaustible determination, for while anything is possible, there is limited time in which to do it. Tireless determination, of course, is not always easy to nurture in one's self or one's friends. But we can take heart in the fact that with no single correct beginning, and no single correct end, even though there is little time, if we try, nothing we do is a waste of it.

---

96 In *In Defense of Lost Causes* (London: Verso, 2008, 210), Slavoj Žižek quotes from Samuel Beckett's 1983 novel *Worstward Ho*: "Try again. Fail again. Fail better." Unfortunately, this often gets used as a new age self-help mantra, but Žižek means something more like Beckett did, if with a more "hopeful" spin (Beckett was not big on hope). Failure is not struggle gone wrong; failure is all there is. This is a much tougher lesson than "if at first you don't succeed, try, try again."

Index

M

ABOUT THE AUTHOR

Geoff Mann is the director of the Centre for Global Political Economy at Simon Fraser University, where he is a member of the Department of Geography. His teaching and research focus on the political economy of contemporary capitalism, with a special emphasis on the power and politics of macroeconomic policy in Europe and North America. He has contributed to *New Left Review*, *Historical Materialism*, and *Antipode* (among other publications), and his book, *Our Daily Bread: Wages, Workers and the Political Economy of the American West* (UNC, 2007), won the American Political Science Association's Michael Harrington Prize and the American Sociological Association's Paul Sweezy Prize. He is currently writing a book on the many lives of Keynesianism. Geoff has a long association with the Dogwood Initiative, a NGO based in Victoria, BC, and with the BC office of the Canadian Centre for Policy Alternatives. He and his partner Michelle and their sons Finn and Seamus live, obsess about soccer, and cook up a lot of excellent Mexican food right near Trout Lake Park in East Vancouver.

ABOUT AK PRESS

AK Press is one of the world's largest and most productive anarchist publishing houses. We're entirely worker-run and democratically managed. We operate without a corporate structure—no boss, no managers, no bullshit. We publish close to twenty books every year, and distribute thousands of other titles published by other like-minded independent presses from around the globe.

The Friends of AK program is a way that you can directly contribute to the continued existence of AK Press, and ensure that we're able to keep publishing great books just like this one! Friends pay $25 a month directly into our publishing account ($30 for Canada, $35 for international), and receive a copy of every book AK Press publishes for the duration of their membership! Friends also receive a discount on anything they order from our website or buy at a table: 50% on AK titles, and 20% on everything else. We've also added a new Friends of AK ebook program: $15 a month gets you an electronic copy of every book we publish for the duration of your membership. Combine it with a print subscription, too!

There's great stuff in the works—so sign up now to become a Friend of AK Press, and let the presses roll!

Email friendsofak@akpress.org for more info, or visit the Friends of AK Press website:
www.akpress.org/programs/friendsofak

PRAISE FOR
DISASSEMBLY REQUIRED

"A brilliantly lucid book. Mann illuminates the basic principles of modern capitalism, their expressions in contemporary economies and states, and their devastating socio-ecological consequences for working people everywhere. This is a must-read if we are to envision ways of organizing our common planetary existence that are not based upon the illusory promises of market fundamentalism and the suicidal ideology of endless economic growth."—**Neil Brenner**, *New State Spaces*

"Geoff Mann is a new breed of monkey-wrencher. He knows that contemporary capitalism has a perverse habit of dismantling itself and gives us a toolkit to build a new, more socially just edifice."—**Andy Merrifield**, *Magical Marxism*

"Insightful and incisive, thoughtful and thorough, filled with new avenues for thinking about resistence. Pass this one by at your own peril."—**Matt Hern**, *Common Ground in a Liquid City*

"An essential handbook for understanding 'actually existing' capitalism, and thus the world as it really is—rather than as it is theorized and justified by the dissembling high priests of mainstream academia, policy, and politics."—**Christian Parenti**, *Tropic of Chaos*